George Tesar
Editor

T0358733

International Business Teaching in Eastern and Central European Countries

International Business Teaching in Eastern and Central European Countries has been co-published simultaneously as *Journal of Teaching in International Business*, Volume 13, Numbers 3/4 2002.

*Pre-publication
REVIEWS,
COMMENTARIES,
EVALUATIONS . . .*

" A SIGNIFICANT CONTRIBUTION
to the field."

Marie Pribova, PhD
*Professor of Marketing
Graduate School of Business
Czech Management Center
Celakovice, Czech Republic*

International Business Press
An Imprint of The Haworth Press, Inc.

International
Business Teaching
in Eastern and Central
European Countries

International Business Teaching in Eastern and Central European Countries has been co-published simultaneously as *Journal of Teaching in International Business*, Volume 13, Numbers 3/4 2002.

The *Journal of Teaching in International Business* Monographic "Separates"

Below is a list of "separates," which in serials librarianship means a special issue simultaneously published as a special journal issue or double-issue *and* as a "separate" hardbound monograph. (This is a format which we also call a "DocuSerial.")

"Separates" are published because specialized libraries or professionals may wish to purchase a specific thematic issue by itself in a format which can be separately cataloged and shelved, as opposed to purchasing the journal on an on-going basis. Faculty members may also more easily consider a "separate" for classroom adoption.

"Separates" are carefully classified separately with the major book jobbers so that the journal tie-in can be noted on new book order slips to avoid duplicate purchasing.

You may wish to visit Haworth's website at . . .

http://www.HaworthPress.com

. . . to search our online catalog for complete tables of contents of these separates and related publications.

You may also call 1-800-HAWORTH (outside US/Canada: 607-722-5857), or Fax 1-800-895-0582 (outside US/Canada: 607-771-0012), or e-mail at:

getinfo@haworthpressinc.com

International Business Teaching in Eastern and Central European Countries, edited by George Tesar (Vol. 13, No. 3/4, 2002). *"IMPORTANT . . . OFFERS UNIQUE AND CURRENT INSIGHTS." (Jerome K. Laurent, PhD, Professor of Economics, University of Wisconsin-Whitewater)*

Management Education in the Chinese Setting, edited by Alma Whiteley (Vol. 12, No. 2, 2001). *"Explores the challenges and opportunities that Greater China offers to educators in program and course development, delivery of programs and other materials, and the development of instructors."*

Teaching International Business: Ethics and Corporate Social Responsibility, edited by Gopalkrishnan R. Iyer (Vol. 11, No. 1, 1999). *"This book is a collection of academic writings on the issues and challenges of incorporating ethics and corporate social responsibility concerns into international business education. You will find frameworks and approaches detailing various pedagogical issues presented."*

Teaching and Program Variations in International Business, edited by Erdener Kaynak and John R. Schermerhorn, Jr. (Vol. 10, No. 3/4, 1999). *"This informative guide explores new avenues that will assist educators in providing undergraduate and graduate students with important, firsthand experiences in international business. Becoming competitive in today's global market is increasingly difficult, and this book will help you use organizational learning tools, the Internet, and agency accredidations to fully prepare students for a successful career in the international marketplace."*

Business Simulations, Games and Experiential Learning in International Business Education, edited by Joseph Wolfe and J. Bernard Keys (Vol. 8, No. 4, 1997). *"A concise and useful collection of materials that might be used to enhance the effectiveness of international business games and simulations." (Saeed Samiee, Professor of Marketing, College of Business Administration, The University of Tulsa, Tulsa, OK)*

The Teaching of Organizational Behavior Across Discipline and National Boundaries: A Role for Information Technology, edited by Alma M. Whiteley (Vol. 7, No. 4, 1996). *"Makes an important contribution to the teaching of organizational behavior by contributing to our understanding of the process by which the effectiveness can be enhanced by group processes, both in educational and strategy development contexts. This is a text for the bookshelf of every business school teacher irrespective of discipline." (David McHardy Reid, PhD, Director, Citicorp Doctoral Programme, School of Business, University of Hong Kong)*

Central and Eastern Europe and the CIS, edited by Jerome Witt (Vol. 7, No. 2, 1996). *"A good overview of the problems of Western-generated reform efforts to business and economic education in the transnational economies of Central and Eastern Europe and the CIS." (Earl Molander, Professor, School of Business Administration, Portland State University)*

Internationalization of the Business Curriculum, edited by Manton C. Gibbs, Jr. (Vol. 5, No. 3, 1994). *"A timely masterpiece which is one step ahead of other books of its kind. . . . Invaluable for university administrators, faculty and business students, industry practitioners, corporate planners, and policymakers." (Jaideep Motwani, PhD, Assistant Professor of Management, Grand Valley State University)*

Environmental Issues in the Curricula of International Business: The Green Imperative, edited by Alma T. Mintu-Wimsatt, Héctor R. Lozada, and Michael J. Polonsky (Vol. 5, No. 1/2, 1994). *"One of the first attempts to make international business academics aware of environmental issues. . . . Contains interdiscplinary information that will appeal to a diverse audience including researchers, practitioners, policymakers, and students." (Journal of Asian Business)*

Utilizing New Information Technology in Teaching of International Business: A Guide for Instructors, edited by Fahri Karakaya and Erdener Kaynak (Vol. 4, No. 3/4, 1993). *"Concise . . . This volume offers a series of evaluators of the latest computer information techniques and tools with an eye to their utility as teaching tools . . . written from a user's perspective. . . . Offers the instructor quick access to information about the new information technologies available." (Ronald S. Rubin, Professor of Marketing, University of Central Florida)*

International Business Teaching in Eastern and Central European Countries

George Tesar, PhD
Editor

International Business Teaching in Eastern and Central European Countries has been co-published simultaneously as *Journal of Teaching in International Business*, Volume 13, Numbers 3/4 2002.

Routledge
Taylor & Francis Group

LONDON AND NEW YORK

First published 2002 by The Haworth Press, Inc.

2 Park Square, Milton Park, Abingdon, Oxfordshire OX14 4RN
605 Third Avenue, New York, NY 10017

Routledge is an imprint of the Taylor & Francis Group, an informa business

First issued in hardback 2020

International Business Teaching in Eastern and Central European Countries has been co-published simultaneously as *Journal of Teaching in International Business*, Volume 13, Numbers 3/4 2002.

Cover design by Marylouise Doyle

Library of Congress Cataloging-in-Publication Data

International business teaching in Eastern and Central European countries / George Tesar, editor.
    p. cm.
    "International business teaching in Eastern and Central European countries has been co-published simultaneously as the Journal of teaching in international business, volume 13, numbers 3/4 2002."
    Includes bibliographical references and index.
    ISBN 0-7890-1952-3 (hard : alk. paper)–ISBN 0-7890-1953-1 (pbk : alk. paper)
    1. Business education–Europe, Eastern. I. Tesar, George. II. Journal of teaching in international business
HF1165.E852 I58 2002
650'.071'047–dc21
                                                                    2002012845

ISBN 13: 978-0-7890-1952-3 (hbk)
ISBN 13: 978-0-7890-1953-0 (pbk)

Indexing, Abstracting & Website/Internet Coverage

This section provides you with a list of major indexing & abstracting services. That is to say, each service began covering this periodical during the year noted in the right column. Most Websites which are listed below have indicated that they will either post, disseminate, compile, archive, cite or alert their own Website users with research-based content from this work. (This list is as current as the copyright date of this publication.)

(continued)

Special Bibliographic Notes related to special journal issues (separates) and indexing/abstracting:

- indexing/abstracting services in this list will also cover material in any "separate" that is co-published simultaneously with Haworth's special thematic journal issue or DocuSerial. Indexing/abstracting usually covers material at the article/chapter level.
- monographic co-editions are intended for either non-subscribers or libraries which intend to purchase a second copy for their circulating collections.
- monographic co-editions are reported to all jobbers/wholesalers/approval plans. The source journal is listed as the "series" to assist the prevention of duplicate purchasing in the same manner utilized for books-in-series.
- to facilitate user/access services all indexing/abstracting services are encouraged to utilize the co-indexing entry note indicated at the bottom of the first page of each article/chapter/contribution.
- this is intended to assist a library user of any reference tool (whether print, electronic, online, or CD-ROM) to locate the monographic version if the library has purchased this version but not a subscription to the source journal.
- individual articles/chapters in any Haworth publication are also available through the Haworth Document Delivery Service (HDDS).

International Business Teaching in Eastern and Central European Countries

CONTENTS

ABOUT THE EDITOR

George Tesar, PhD, (University of Wisconsin), is Professor of Marketing and International Business at the Umeå School of Business and Economics, Umeå University, Sweden. He was previously Professor of Marketing at the University of Wisconsin, Whitewater. Dr. Tesar is also a senior marketing specialist and an international consultant to top management in the high technology, automotive, and consumer product industries in North America, Europe, and Southeast Asia.

Over the past ten years, Dr. Tesar has been active in Europe as a management education and training specialist for a number of private firms and public institutions. He specializes in bridging managerial styles and practices between Central and Eastern Europe and the West. In his practice, Dr. Tesar offers a range of services, including assessment of global marketing opportunities, technology transfer management, product development strategies, and marketing research studies along with cross-cultural training between Central European and Western managers.

Preface

I am very pleased to offer this special volume devoted to international business teaching in Eastern and Central European countries. Professor George Tesar of University of Umeå, Sweden is to be congratulated for bringing this outstanding special publication to fruition. There are curriculum, teaching, and program-related articles written by authors who come from the area countries. The very insightful articles offered in this volume will make an excellent contribution to the area of business administration teaching research and would find enthusiastic support among *JTIB* readership.

The paper by Denton Marks examines the role and content of MBA programs in major universities in transitional economies of Central and Eastern Europe that are free of inertia of traditional programs in Western universities. It stipulates that rethinking fundamental principles in offering MBA programs contributes to the introduction of new programs that are both efficient and appropriate for the emerging economics systems they will serve. Enterprises in transition economies have an advantage in adopting technology that has already been tested and proven by others because the educational programs can benefit by choosing from the best of what has been developed in the rest of the world. The discussion in this paper considers a number of choices that economists face in providing instruction in economics as a part of an MBA program. MBA students and future managers need to develop an understanding of how economics, and more specifically resource allocation concepts, impact their future abilities as managers.

The presentation by Cannon, Yaprak and Mokra describes a simulation game designed to help students in transformation economies understand the impact of various government intervention strategies on

[Haworth co-indexing entry note]: "Preface." Kaynak, Erdener. Co-published simultaneously in *Journal of Teaching in International Business* (International Business Press, an imprint of The Haworth Press, Inc.) Vol. 13, No. 3/4, 2002, pp. xvii-xx and: *International Business Teaching in Eastern and Central European Countries* (ed: George Tesar) International Business Press, an imprint of The Haworth Press, Inc., 2002, pp. xiii-xvi. Single or multiple copies of this article are available for a fee from The Haworth Document Delivery Service [1-800-HAWORTH 9:00 a.m. - 5:00 p.m. (EST). E-mail address: getinfo@haworthpressinc.com].

the free market system. Students can take an individual economic entity that is able to contribute labor, consumer goods, and acquire wealth. The students have the opportunity to participate in three different types of economies. The three economies provide a conceptual foundation for a fundamental understanding of how various governmental interventions combined with other governmental action impacts the free market system and economic development. This simulation game is important in training future managers to understand different forms of governmental intervention and how they impact managers' ability to make rational decisions in different economies. The particular focus in this presentation is on import substitution and export promotion as two contrasting strategies of economic development.

The differences in teaching business courses with the use of cases in Central and Eastern Europe (CEE) and the United States (US) is contrasted in the paper by Tom Bramorski. The reasons why these differences exist are explored in depth and are supplemented by the author's experiences in teaching in both systems. The differences between methodology and content of teaching business programs in CEE and the US are largely due to cultural differences, according to the author. Business programs in the US are more structured and designed to enhance the student's professional career; business programs in CEE are less structured and frequently lack systematic organization. The use of cases in connecting the content of the course with the real business environment also differs significantly in the two systems. Cases used in CEE business programs tend to provide a basis for descriptive in-class discussions, while in the US, the courses are used to develop a better understanding of concepts and help students as future managers learn how to deal with adverse situations and make sound decisions. The author suggests that there is strong demand for business programs throughout CEE, but a relatively low supply of quality programs and the use of cases tends to be minimal.

The implications for ineffective learning by business students in CEE who are trying to create vibrant private sectors are large. The paper by Zapalska and Perry presents the details of a collaborative learning instrument that can be used in business education in CEE countries and discusses the nature and importance of entrepreneurial education in business courses. A theoretical justification for using a collaborative instrument is identified. The instrument and methods of implementation are then outlined, followed by an evaluation of the usefulness of the collaborative learning instrument. Entrepreneurship as a field in college education, according to the authors, is a relatively young discipline. The key element in entrepreneurial education is that all students understand why entrepreneurs are important to the economy of any country. The purpose of entrepreneurial education is to prepare students for career success and to increase their capability for future learning. Collaborative learning in the college classroom is an approach that has been strongly advocated and used to promote educational goals in teaching entrepreneurial issues. Providing a background on the role of entrepreneurship in an enterprise economy is a critical starting point for students from the CEE.

An important aspect of educational reform in CEE is the effort to educate college professors about student learning styles. College professors' understanding of how students learn is an important part of selecting appropriate teaching strategies since knowledge about students' learning styles can assist college professors in adjusting their teaching styles. The paper by Zapalska and Dabb describes an assessment instrument that college professors can use to identify their own teaching strategies as well as to help their students become more aware of their own learning strategies and motivation for learning. College professors in CEE need to know more about differences in learning styles and the complexities of the learning process of their students in order to teach more effectively.

The paper by Miroslav Rebernik demonstrates how an effective university-level business education program can be organized. The focus is on students of business education intending to be employed by small and medium-sized companies in CEE. Part of the philosophy of this program is that students should have an opportunity to experience various strategic and operational functions. The fundamental objective of this program is to produce graduates who can manage small and medium-sized companies or undertake other entrepreneurial positions immediately after graduation from a university level program without needing a lengthy period of adjustment to the business environment and the enterprise. A student internship with a company is an integral component of the program. Each student is assigned to a small or medium-sized company and is expected to function as an employee during the term of the internship. The management of the company is expected to provide sufficient feedback for the student.

The main objective of the paper by Kelemen et al. is to examine management education specifically in Moldova, one of the former republics of the Soviet Union. It proposes that economic reforms must be closely followed by appropriate reforms in management education. The use of networking in creating local management knowledge is essential. The networking approach requires some form of association between interested actors such as business schools, universities, the business community, government agencies, foreign donors, and professional agencies, among others. Such loosely structured networks can enable interested parties to stay in touch and be informed about each other's activities, interest, and problems. The Moldavian International Institute of Management, described by the authors, was established as a result of networking.

The paper by Kerkovsky, Janicek and Drdla provides an overview of MBA education in the Czech Republic. MBA education is not broadly accepted in the Czech Republic and faces a number of systemic obstacles ranging from acceptance as a valid form of education to simply a general lack of understanding of what an MBA program represents for future managers. The Czech Association of MBA Schools and its responsibilities are also described. A summary of the experiences of individuals directly involved with the development of an MBA program at one of the major universities in the Czech Republic are included in the paper as are suggestions for development of similar programs. The authors conclude that the foundation for management education, and especially MBA level education, is very strong in the Czech Republic.

May I take this opportunity to thank George Tesar very much for his diligence and hard work for the completion of this volume. As well, contributors to the volume are to be congratulated for their hard work and perseverance. It is a volume of significant importance which will be welcome reading material for readers of *Journal of Teaching in International Business*.

Have a happy and enjoyable reading!

Erdener Kaynak

Introduction

Educational opportunities in Central and Eastern Europe have changed dramatically over the past twelve-year period. Restructuring of undergraduate and graduate programs has required systematic rethinking of programs, courses, and teaching methods. Post-graduate education, particularly professional education and especially management education, has evolved as one of the most important elements impacting the political, social, and economic changes in that part of the world.

There was a dramatic need for new educational programs in business, but there was also a need for changes in the content of the courses being offered at the beginning of the transition. Along with the course content changes there was, and in some cases there still is, a need to change teaching staff's perceptions as to how students learn and retain their knowledge.

Many teaching professionals and university professors from the West volunteered their services for a variety of programs. Major grants became available from Western governments to revise and improve curricula at major universities in Central and Eastern Europe and, in several cases, establish new opportunities for undergraduate and graduate business education such as the International Management Center in Budapest, CMC Graduate School of Business near Prague, and the American University in Bulgaria. Central and Eastern European educators also contributed greatly to the development and implementation of better and more relevant approaches to teaching in many of the business disciplines.

The purpose of this special double volume is to focus on some of the developments that have emerged over the past twelve years and highlight those developments that have played a significant role in improv-

[Haworth co-indexing entry note]: "Introduction." Tesar, George. Co-published simultaneously in *Journal of Teaching in International Business* (International Business Press, an imprint of The Haworth Press, Inc.) Vol. 13, No. 3/4, 2002, pp. 1-3; and: *International Business Teaching in Eastern and Central European Countries* (ed: George Tesar) International Business Press, an imprint of The Haworth Press, Inc., 2002, pp. 1-3. Single or multiple copies of this article are available for a fee from The Haworth Document Delivery Service [1-800-HAWORTH 9:00 a.m. - 5:00 p.m. (EST). E-mail address: getinfo@haworthpressinc.com].

ing business education in Central and Eastern Europe. The initial call for contributions to this special double volume generated an enormous number of manuscripts. Seventeen reviewers from eight countries contributed their time to review these manuscripts. A large number of these manuscripts came from Central and Eastern Europe. Some were accepted for publication, however, most of them were rejected. The typical reason for rejection was a lack of methodology, the lack of a concept, or a lack of relevancy to teaching of business concepts.

The overall perspective that emerged from this experience suggests that there are four areas that are still extremely important to teaching of the business concepts in Central and Eastern Europe. They are: (1) the general notion of economics and its use in business, specifically in management (for example, the contribution by Denton Marks); (2) the use of decision-making tools and cases in communicating importance of business concepts and their use (as demonstrated by Hugh Cannon and his colleagues and by Tom Bramorski); (3) the importance of learning about learning in Central and Eastern Europe (as outlined by Alina Zapalska and her colleagues); and (4) graduate education in general, especially MBA education (discussed by Miloslav Kerkovsky and his colleagues).

The concepts outlined above provide an interesting insight into how teaching of business is carried out in that part of the world, how it is structured, and what some of the important issues are in educating future managers in Central and Eastern Europe. In conclusion, this special volume provides a unique perspective into several approaches designed to improve business education in that part of the world in order to stimulate growth and competition in the local markets. The following reviewers helped to highlight these concepts for this special double volume. As a Special editor, I want to thank them for their efforts in helping authors improve their contributions. They are:

> Håkan Boter, Umeå University
> Tom Bramorski, University of Wisconsin-Whitewater
> Petr Chardraba, DePaul University
> James D. Goodnow, Bradley University
> Andrew C. Gross, Cleveland State University
> Stephen J. Havlovic, University of Wisconsin-Whitewater
> Miroslav Keřkovský, Brno University of Technology
> Jorma Larimo, University of Vaasa
> Jerome K. Laurent, University of Wisconsin-Whitewater

Marin Marinov, Gloucestershire Business School
Denton Marks, University of Wisconsin-Whitewater
Klaus E. Meyer, Copenhagen Business School
Hamid Moini, University of Wisconsin-Whitewater
Jan Nowak, University of New Brunswick
Marie Příbová, CMC Graduate School of Business
Paul Thistlethwaite, Western Illinois University
Timothy Wilson, Clarion University

Thank you again

George Tesar, PhD (Wisconsin)
Umeå School of Business and Economics
Umeå University
Umeå, Sweden

The Role of Economics
in the Management Curriculum:
An Analysis for the Transition Economies

Denton Marks

SUMMARY. The economic transition in the Central and Eastern European Countries provides a unique opportunity to observe the evolution of economies from planned systems to more market-oriented and decentralized systems. Aside from the bounty of economic policy issues raised by such a transition, a more fundamental adjustment involves the design of education for the future managers in these economies and, in particular, the role of economics–a subject at the core of the transition–in the management curriculum. Using the MBA curriculum as its focus, this paper discusses both the rationale for including economics in the program for various curricular models and the particular relevance of the subject to management students in the transition environment. *[Article copies available for a fee from The Haworth Document Delivery Service: 1-800-HAWORTH. E-mail address: <getinfo@haworthpressinc.com> Website: <http://www.HaworthPress.com> © 2002 by The Haworth Press, Inc. All rights reserved.]*

Denton Marks is Professor of Economics, University of Wisconsin-Whitewater, Whitewater, WI 53190 (E-mail: marksd@uwwvax.uww.edu).

An early version of this paper was presented at the Session on Management Education in the CEEC, 18th World Congress of the Czechoslovak Society of Arts and Sciences (August, 1996) in Brno, Czech Republic.

[Haworth co-indexing entry note]: "The Role of Economics in the Management Curriculum: An Analysis for the Transition Economies." Marks, Denton. Co-published simultaneously in *Journal of Teaching in International Business* (International Business Press, an imprint of The Haworth Press, Inc.) Vol. 13, No. 3/4, 2002, pp. 5-21; and: *International Business Teaching in Eastern and Central European Countries* (ed: George Tesar) International Business Press, an imprint of The Haworth Press, Inc., 2002, pp. 5-21. Single or multiple copies of this article are available for a fee from The Haworth Document Delivery Service [1-800-HAWORTH 9:00 a.m. - 5:00 p.m. (EST). E-mail address: getinfo@haworthpressinc.com].

KEYWORDS. Economics, management education, transition economies, CEEC

INTRODUCTION

The world's economists have had a particular interest in events in Central and Eastern Europe and the former Soviet Union over the last decade. The analysis of the actual and proper transition of former planned economies into some form of more market-oriented economy has been an intellectual "growth industry" for the economics profession. Since so much of an economist's expertise draws upon or assumes a certain institutional arrangement for a given economy, changes in the basic structure of several major industrial economies elicits reaction from every field of the profession.

One could anticipate the focus of most of the economic research on the "transition economies" (TE): the pros and cons of markets, how domestic markets might emerge in economies that heretofore have been populated largely by state-owned enterprises (SOE) producing to plan largely for domestic consumers, the introduction or reform of institutions essential to the operation of a more market-oriented economy (e.g., financial institutions such as banks), the development of policies that allow significant but much curtailed government management of the economy (e.g., monetary and fiscal policy) (e.g., Blanchard, Froot, and Sachs, 1994). In contrast, the focus here is less obvious but perhaps more fundamental. The structural direction taken by transition economies depends upon political processes and their stability, the respect for laws passed, and the timing and depth of the structural changes initiated. The success and persistence of such changes depends upon the resulting economic performance, which, in turn, depends upon how the economies' decision makers alter their behavior. One critical class of decision makers is business managers. This paper focuses upon their formal training and how it can facilitate their adaptation to a more market-oriented economy.

THE SETTING

Macroeconomic and industry-specific policy analyses and prescriptions for transition economies are more plentiful than serious discussions of the educational challenges that economic transition entails.

However, writing about a conceptual model of the transformation of Central and Eastern European (CEE) economies from command economy to market economy, one author has highlighted the "relearning" that enterprise managers must undertake:

> Western analysts' observation of managers accustomed to operating under socialist principles calls for a transformation in managerial behavior. Thus, managers should be trained in the areas of taking responsibility for decision-making and risk taking. They should learn to assess market opportunities, obtain and invest capital in productive projects, use information systems, cash-flow management, and standard systems of accounting. Most importantly, training programs should be designed to make managerial attitudes and behaviors compatible with the goals specified above [i.e., customer orientation, self-reliance and independence from government subsidies, lean and flexible organizational structure, total quality management, and innovation]. (Culpan, 1995: 8)

We might disagree about the details of the prescription that flows from concerns about the preparedness of enterprise managers emerging from command economies, but we are unlikely to disagree about the need for a change in management orientation. Others have provided more thorough and focused analyses of the new elements of management training needed (e.g., Kasperson and Dobrzynbski, 1995; Tesar, 1995). One study of Hungarian medium and upper level managers using a management simulation model identified the following characteristics of their management style: equate capacity with demand, fear debt, hoard cash, undervalue market information, price products erratically, view the competitive process as static, view the dimensions of competition narrowly, disregard social responsibility (Ullman, 1995: 143-6). The descriptions could apply as well to undergraduate business students at a North American university who have had textbook training but no significant experience as decision makers in a market –but then that also describes the Hungarian managers.

A review of "Western" business programs would reveal that their faculties assume that a comprehensive program to train professional managers needs a significant module on market economics. However, a number of issues arise in designing that module; some are unique to the context of transition economies, and some apply to any business curriculum. A benefit from such a module particularly apparent for transition economies is exposure to the principles underlying the economic systems that prevail in most of the world.

A number of premises underlie the discussion that follows. First, we assume that the economy in which the manager, or management student, operates experiences structural changes which alter the fundamental domestic allocative mechanism from central (government) planning and control to markets populated by decentralized decision makers (consumers, producers). Second, the change in structure necessitates a fundamental shift in the enterprise's goals (e.g., customer satisfaction, self-reliance) and, in turn, the manager's behavior. Of particular importance are the new roles for decentralized consumer and producer decision making, the greatly expanded benefits and risks from making choices, and the new priority of consumer sovereignty as the ultimate arbiter of the economy's direction: production exists ultimately to serve the consumer whose happiness is the ultimate goal of the economy.

Third, the economy's system of education will have a profound effect upon the nature of any national economic "transition"; beyond the family (and perhaps the church), the system of formal education is the social institution to which citizens turn to develop future human resources.

The fourth premise is one of the most tenuous: formal management training is the most effective method of developing management rapidly; and, in particular, programs such as a traditional Masters of Business Administration (MBA) post-baccalaureate program are particularly effective at producing better managers. Finally, if we acknowledge the importance of an MBA program, then we must determine the role that economics training plays in that program. (While the discussion takes a conventional MBA program as its focus, most of the ideas apply to any career-oriented business program pursued after an initial general education program at the university level.)

In this discussion, a course in the principles of economics will mean that course or module taught in most undergraduate management or MBA programs in industrialized economies in the Americas, Europe, and Asia. This will be termed "market economics" (ME).

ECONOMICS AND THE MBA CURRICULUM

The emergence of MBA programs in major universities in transition economies provides a unique opportunity to examine the role and content of such programs free from the inertia of traditional programs in Western universities. Re-thinking fundamental principles contributes to the introduction of new programs that are both efficient and appropriate for the emerging economic systems they will serve. Just as some have recognized the advantage that enterprises in transition economies have in adopting technology that has already been tested and proven by others–much like the advantage German and Japanese firms had after World War II (Culpan, 1995: 11)–educational programs can benefit by choosing from the best of what has been developed in the rest of the world.

Questions about teaching economics may seem more like education problems than allocation problems. However, they in fact involve questions of resource allocation: What is the rationale for including instruction in economics in an MBA program to the exclusion of something else and, once included, what should an ME course contain? This discussion considers a number of choices that economists face in providing this instruction.

They fall into three categories–the program, the students, and course content.

Culture-specific challenges also arise from the classroom process–grading, method of instruction and testing, teaching evaluations–but these are not considered here.

THE PROGRAM

Consider three perspectives on the role of economics in a curriculum: the requirements of the curricular model adopted, professional ("expert") opinion on worthy educational programs, and the market test. The last is now newly important in transition economies because labor, including managerial talent, will increasingly be allocated by the forces of supply and demand if these economies truly embrace a market system. Whereas managers in these economies were formerly assigned to their positions in the spirit of "capacity equals demand," educational programs must now consider the skills that employers want as they design their curriculum.

Underlying this analysis is the educational institution's goal of providing a program, which will operate at (perhaps growing) capacity. Whether it approaches this goal in response to a bureaucratic mandate or, at the other extreme, to maximize its profits (revenues less costs), we assume that it aims to offer a program that will enroll and eventually graduate students. While the idea of operating a university as a business raises a number of troubling issues (Marks, 1998b), it is not unusual for administrators to operate at least some programs within the university such as an MBA program much like "profit centers."

Such programs may exist for a number of reasons, only a few of which appear in university catalogs. We can identify four models–instrumentalism, signaling, grooming, and barrier to entry. While any given program may reflect all of these models, most reflect most clearly only one or two.

The most common stated purpose of such a program is to impart to those interested in a management career (usually private sector and for-profit) a set of skills that are either almost exclusively available in a classroom (perhaps including internet) setting or attainable elsewhere only with an extended period of on-the-job experience, presumably at greater cost. A representative statement of the objectives of an MBA-level graduate business program is:

> to provide sound preparation in foundation courses concerning basic tools and functional areas that are critical to understanding business,
>
> to study in depth those tools and functional areas that are essential to sound administrative practices,
>
> to provide tools and knowledge for identifying problems, collecting and analyzing data to make sound decisions in a dynamic economic environment.
>
> (UW-Whitewater, 1992: 2)

Another typical curriculum operates two MBA programs, one of which resembles the one just described and which emphasizes "concentrated exposure to a specific field of Business study and development of applied research skills" (Simon Fraser University, 1990: 256). This approach suggests "instrumentalism" ("Tools")–the provision of analytic skills or tools–as its focus. It is the most common perception of MBA programs and the one most readily embraced by those developing new programs.

Other possible models include labor market signaling ("Signal") as explained by Spence (1973) –the particular content of the program is subordinate to its role as a filter in helping buyers (employers) identify the quality (e.g., innate ability) of the graduates available. The intellectual tools developed through the curriculum are less important than the hurdles cleared by the students–whether intellectual, psychological, or social.

A third model is acclimatization and socialization–the program grooms individuals to enter the world of upper management and imparts more "tricks of the trade" than true academic training. A course in corporate protocol may be more important than one in corporate finance. A Canadian program for mid-career managers and executives that provides "a generalized course of studies which exposes the student to broad management issues rather than in-depth specialization within business subjects" (Simon Fraser University, 1990: 256) might reflect this orientation. This is the idea of grooming managers ("Grooming").

Yet another model could be the erection of an unofficial barrier to entry to upper management to enhance the status and incomes of degree holders ("Barrier"). The lack of control over supply into those echelons which seem to determine entry more on the basis of past business experience and performance than academic credentials weakens the argument, but some (e.g., business schools and their alumni) might promote such a possibility. Also, individuals with such degrees have an incentive to promote their importance. If this is not an issue for professional education in transition economies, it may become one as potential market rewards increase for professional managers. The particular economic content of the curriculum has little impact upon its role as a barrier to entry except to the extent that the other models create barriers as a by-product. For example, as a Tool or Signal, economics is a relatively technical management subject that most students find challenging; competence in it therefore represents an obstacle that many actual and potential students have difficulty surmounting. However, its justification in those models is not as a barrier *per se*. Therefore, because it has no particular value in creating barriers, this model will not be discussed further.

What role can economics play in these curricular models? Relatively technical analytic skills (e.g., statistical analysis, mathematical modeling) are relevant to numerous management functions so that a Tools rationale warrants some exposure to ME. This would seem particularly compelling for transition economies (e.g., Marks, 2000). Managers there need to be among the first to appreciate the fundamental significance of property rights, market-determined prices, macroeconomic management, the competitive process and "survival of the fittest", the preeminence of the consumer–even the process of rent-seeking ("the economics of special interest lobbying"), although it probably transcends economic systems (e.g., Lazear, 1995). While the choice in course emphasis between development of analytic skills ("thinking like an economist") and broad exposure to economic issues is important (see below), it is subordinate to the more obviously beneficial role of somehow including ME in the curriculum.

An aptitude for economic analysis may be a valuable signal to potential employers. Skill in technical subjects such as statistics, mathematics, and engineering, which currently occupy a central place in CEE management curricula, may reflect a similar aptitude, but the behavioral and policy analytic content of economics as well its emphasis upon the discovery of counterintuitive results and unintended consequences of decision making means that it can play a distinct role in identifying potential management skill. Thus, the role of ME in a Signal curriculum suggests a role for ME courses, which emphasize "thinking like an economist." While currently missing as a focus in universities so recently controlled by socialist regimes, a Grooming curriculum might prefer a cursory exposure to a broad range of economic ideas and issues in contrast to the development of analytic skills and a relatively strong emphasis on both establishing contacts with business, government, and academic celebrities and exploiting the associations and relationships flowing from such professional and social networks.

A second basis for determining the proper role of ME is simply economists' perception of the vocational value added of training in ME to non-economists–reliance upon "expert opinion." The profession would express a variety of opinions about the vocational value of such training. At one extreme are those whose pursuit of the subject is purely academic and for whom any practical implications are an occasional and unintentional by-product; specialists in advanced theory come to mind. At the other extreme are non-academic practitioners applying methods such as cost-benefit analysis, forecasting, and forensic analysis (e.g., economic analysis supporting civil litigation) who would support teaching these more obviously marketable skills. However, support for the vocational value of training need not be this narrow. Many feel that simply learning to "think like an economist" is the valuable skill aside from any interest in becoming an economist:

> A broad consensus exists among economics faculty that enabling students to "think like an economist" is the over-arching goal of economics education. All other virtues follow. . . . Thinking like an economist involves using chains of deductive reasoning in con-

junction with simplified models–such as supply and demand, marginal analysis, benefit-cost analysis, and comparative advantage–to help understand economic phenomena. It involves identifying tradeoffs in the context of constraints, distinguishing positive . . . from normative . . . analysis, tracing the behavioral implications of some change while abstracting from other aspects of reality, and exploring the consequences of aggregation. It also involves describing . . . redistributive implications . . . amassing data to evaluate and refine our understanding . . . and testing alternative hypotheses . . .

Thinking like an economist includes problem-solving and creative thinking . . . an emphasis on parsimonious models . . . fundamental principles of economics . . . thought to be universal . . . decision making techniques . . .

The most coveted economic analysis is that which challenges conventional wisdom, or, in the policymaking context, isolates unintended outcomes. Finally, the specification of "constraints" and the articulation of a strategy to manage best within those constraints involves creative judgment . . .

(Siegfried et al., 1991: 199-201)

This view presents the discipline's role as a method of thinking that would improve one's approach to many types of business problems.

Many CEE managers know related engineering-oriented techniques (e.g., constrained optimization models, linear programming, operations analysis). The goal is introducing economic applications of those technical skills and understanding management with a new "objective function."[1]

Hlavacek provides a model of SOE management behavior particularly relevant here. He models the SOE manager's objective function as maximizing the enterprise's reserve, or the difference between its production capacity and its actual output: ". . . The center determines the plan for the year t as a given percentage increase from the output levels of year $t-1$ . . . a firm that produced as efficiently as possible in year $t-1$ would probably not be able to fulfill the plan for the next year. The manager of such a firm would be replaced by the central authority. That is why managers with an efficiency-minimizing objective function survive . . ." (Hlavacek, 1992: 5). Others have confirmed that "management's main aim was to negotiate a plan which would be easy to meet" (Kerkovsky, 1998: 346). As these characterizations suggest, the challenge may not be that traditional managers are not rational in the economic sense; it is that the planning system encouraged questionable goals, and management training requires more of a change in focus than a change in paradigm.

Finally, if an economist wishes to determine the role her discipline should play in a degree program, she may believe that the market is the best judge. Reliance upon a market test is complicated by the need to identify the relevant market. One view is that the program is producing and selling education. But who is the customer? Is it the student? If so, does the student simply want the most saleable skills in the current marketplace? In the near-future market? In the market spanning her career? This model of the student as upgraded and overhauled machinery may be too superficial; the desires of students are more complex and may involve nonvocational goals. Are potential employers of graduates the customers? Identifying this group and its demands, particularly in a transition economy, is a similarly daunting task. Unfortunately, the information is unclear here; in addition, one may question the extent to which the market should dictate curricular content in a university (e.g., Bloom, 1987).[2] Notwithstanding Adam Smith's preferred approach to pedagogy (i.e., a teacher is judged by her ability to attract students as "buyers"), the nature of higher education is that the faculty as experts should play a significant role in determining what is taught. If students knew what lessons of economics were most valuable to them, then they would not be students.

On the other hand, few academic economists are business people, and yet they hope to address the needs of and motivate employment-oriented students. To some extent, this is a systemic problem with the MBA–academically oriented professors teaching vocationally oriented students (e.g., Murray, 1988). This problem with the MBA curriculum is more difficult than the one we face with North American undergraduate programs where the students' lack of direction and, less commonly, motivation can also be a strength when it manifests itself as openness and "flexible" thinking.

Even if this discussion leaves us knowing that ME belongs in the MBA curriculum, we must confront another fundamental question: drawing upon an analogy first suggested by Milton Friedman, if the pool player does not need to know the laws of physics to be an expert player, then does the manager need to know the principles of economics to be most effective? But the question is not limited to training in economics: Do the formal training and MBA credential actually signal any greater productivity? Even if one can act "as if" one knows the relevant principles without the training, there may be some acceleration of development and sharpening of one's skills through formal training. Moreover, one of the greatest values of training in economics is an increased ability to understand economists and to think critically about what they say. It is also worth noting that those who have studied the "credentialing effect"–that credentials serve primarily as barriers to entry without reflecting increased productivity of their holders and that there has been "credential inflation" in recent years–have found that, on average, credentials actually do reflect greater productivity and that employment that has upgraded its credential requirements does in fact demand increased skill (Filer, Hamermesh, and Rees, 1996: 109).

THE STUDENTS

It is not surprising that business students in the CEEC differ from their Western counterparts in their career preparation and that these differences affect curriculum design. Because the rationing of higher education has ostensibly been based more upon merit than price, entry into higher education has been more selective and programs have been more demanding in the CEEC certainly than in North America either at the undergraduate or the graduate or professional level. Moreover, for those attending university, secondary school has provided more rigorous training perhaps because, for most secondary school students, formal education ends there. Few students pursue university training only because their parents insist upon it or because they hope to postpone earning a living. With this background, CEE students are more prepared in some ways to pursue a relatively demanding university curriculum.

On the other hand, these students lack as many and as varied indigenous role models of successful private sector managers. They are learning about management in an economic system quite different from the one in which they grew up and which they will play a significant role in shaping. Not surprisingly, their potential mentors–both those whose management careers straddle the former system and the transition and those who began their careers during the transition–are themselves still making the adjustment and with some difficulty (e.g., Soulsby, 1998). The best models of the organizations to which they aspire in economies which theirs might selectively emulate are elsewhere, but they have demonstrated relatively little interest in venturing beyond their home countries, perhaps because of cost and perceived more reliable and immediate career opportunities at home (Tesar, 1998).

A more fundamental issue for these students and their training is the uncertain outcome of the transition process. A number of authors have encouraged restraint in anticipating the outcome of the transition process (e.g., Langer, 1998; Marks, 1998a). Like the naive early assumption that Western policy experts could both identify and show the way to the goals of transition (Bosworth and Ofer, 1995), an assumption that formal management training in the CEEC should simply mimic successful programs in Western Europe and North America would be premature. More specifically, the foundation of courses in economics should not rest entirely upon the idea of competitive markets but should emphasize ideas that transcend the particular institutional arrangement of the market system. The "new institutional economics" which recognizes the role of the norms, values, and traditions of the community in its framework would warrant particular emphasis (Marks, 2000). Indeed, one need look no farther than university classrooms in the CEEC and the norms of behavior of business students there to witness attitudes toward competition and cooperation and individual achievement that are distinctly different from those found, for example, in a North American business school.[3] These differences are no doubt reflections of the distinct norms of the larger society that preclude any straightforward march toward a market economy.

One difficulty in evaluating the importance of any discipline to a student is its gestation period. For most, ME is, like other technical subjects, a difficult subject relative to many others. Few seem to appreciate it fully at the time they take it. However, we do not know how many students realize eventually that either some particular technique or the general economic approach to problem solving has served them well in one or more contexts.

The gestation period problem is particularly relevant to economics; it is simply less accessible than many subjects. Siegfried et al. state: ". . . [for the undergraduate major] arguments first made in an introductory course are often not fully grasped until the senior year (or beyond)" (p. 202). Because they are older and often have some business experience, Western MBA students are more likely to know they need to understand ME. CEE business students clearly need to develop an understanding of markets and market-related institutions, and they are both better and worse equipped to value the knowledge. They are better equipped because they tend to be more technically trained and because they may view the subject as a source of insight into emerging institutions, including the market economy itself. On the other hand, they do not experience the market economy daily and may, like American college freshmen, have difficulty relating to many ME ideas.

COURSE CONTENT

The third challenge, reflecting ME's limited share of the curriculum, is the choice of course emphasis between "thinking like an economist" (TLE) and a survey of issues. The former emphasis focuses upon teaching the methods of economists and how they can be applied to actual allocation problems; it presents economics as a management technology (Marks, 2000). The latter is more a description of ME problems and what economists have said about them (including some possible solutions). The former teaches an approach to problem solving while the latter attempts simply to sensitize the student to the economic view of the world (like sensitizing them to ethical issues without teaching them how to address them). The former has less room for consideration of a variety of topics because it requires time for the development of analytic techniques while the latter covers more topics but sacrifices the development of deeper understanding of the economic problem and possible solutions. The former is more Tools and Signal oriented while the latter is more appropriate for a Grooming curriculum.

By assumption, a fundamental goal in teaching is to change students: after they are taught, they should never again look at the world the same way. This transformation may be more sweeping for business students in the midst of an economic transition. This suggests a preference for the TLE approach. The goal is to develop managers' instincts for economic relationships. For example, an ME course should develop in them an appreciation for opportunity cost, marginalism, transactions, equilibrium, and modeling. To accomplish this one must carefully present ME methodology, urge students to use it, and provide enough applications that they grasp the power of this line of thinking.

Experience suggests that analytic skills develop best through frequent encounters and different applications of basic concepts. For example, students learn the power of consumer theory through product demand analysis, incidence and burden analysis of a sales tax, the labor supply model, the consumption-savings model, and so forth. The theory illuminates the importance of product substitutability (real or perceived) and the related potential for monopoly power through advertising and real or perceived product differentiation. It presages parallel techniques in production theory and applications such as tax credits and input substitutability. Elasticity is a related concept rich with business applications.

This in-depth approach develops an appreciation for the subject. Once they have that appreciation, they will know enough to look for more–and perhaps be better equipped to understand it on their own–than if they had a broader but less analytically deep exposure. Economic instinct develops with repeated exposure. "This repetition and apparent redundancy is [sic] essential because "application" of economic principles (in contrast to learning economic "technique") is very difficult to master and requires practice . . ." (Siegfried et al., 1991: 202) However, repetition comes at the expense of exposure to a broader range of techniques and topics. There is too little time to cover all the essential ideas–even as suggested by, say, the chapter headings of a standard ME text. Since the preferred repetition occurs "over an extended period of time and across several courses" (*Ibid.*), instilling TLE is perhaps unrealistic when only one or two economics courses are allowed so that a survey of issues is preferred to a stunted development of analytic skills.

Discussion of more specific course content warrants at least another paper, but it deserves a comment here. Most would agree that students must understand fundamental principles such as scarcity, opportunity cost, and modeling. One then has three options: a micro focus, a macro focus, and some blend. The choice here depends upon what we expect managers to do. Very few become economists. Managers rarely need to do macroeconomics; they are most likely to need to understand how the domestic and international economies are behaving, to be familiar with the meaning of some key concepts, and to have some understanding of the rationale for and likely effects of government monetary or fiscal policy. Moreover, the field of macroeconomics is less settled (Becker, 2000). They are more likely to need to do microeconomics–cost/benefit analysis, analysis of factor markets and their institutions, consumer behavior, financial analysis–or to understand someone else's microeconomic analysis. Moreover, most fields where they may have a special interest are micro–housing, transportation, taxation, agriculture, regulation, industrial organization and strategy. Evidence indicates that developing micro before macro increases students' understanding of economics relative to the reverse sequence (Fizel and Johnson, 1986). While this research does not discover why the sequencing matters, it suggests that working through micro first embeds the principles more effectively with macro reinforcement than the alternative.

THE CHANGING BUSINESS ENVIRONMENT

Given a Tools orientation for most MBA candidates, the desire to provide them with decision making tools may come at the expense of providing them with more subtle but no less important conceptual tools that can equip them better to deal with changes in their business environment. For example, in a transition economy, it is worth dwelling on the meaning and key elements of a market, what causes markets and market failure, as well as more fundamental questions about the role of markets in the economy and even the record of performance of planned economies. Applications that stretch students' perception of the subject should expand their appreciation of "the economic problem" and may change the way they think about human behavior and institutions. For example, "public choice" or rent-seeking behavior is a powerful idea that may alter dramatically their ideas about the efficiency of democracy.

CONCLUSION

Numerous choices surround the inclusion and design of an ME course in an MBA curriculum. The case for inclusion in developing MBA programs at universities in the CEEC is particularly strong because of the importance of developing an understanding of the basic principles of ME among the key decision makers in the economy as it evolves. The case for more specific content depends upon the goals of the particular degree program. The nature of the course to be included depends upon the degree of deference to the "buyer" and the "seller." The market for MBA programs, and their courses, operates in an environment of highly asymmetric information: the faculty often has little experience in the careers for which the students are preparing, and the students have had little exposure to the material the professors teach. Moreover, career opportunities are changing rapidly along with the economic institutions.

Reviewing the choices that surround the inclusion and design of the economic content of the curriculum reminds one of the intellectual challenges that teaching presents. There is a fundamental question of allocating scarce resources. Since there is little more than anecdotal evidence bearing upon the issues raised here for management education during the transition, and since there are no experts, it is difficult to make prescriptions other than be sensitive to the choices and to make them intentionally rather than by accident.

NOTES

1. I have been impressed with the technical backgrounds of my CEE students in both the United States and the Czech Republic; the challenge to me has been communicating how to apply those skills to managerial decisionmaking in a competitive environment.
2. For example, it is not uncommon to hear students, alumni, and even administrators argue for the elimination of requirements from a pre-business or core business curriculum (e.g., calculus) because the subject matter is not used regularly in operating a business; alumni may be particularly persuasive in this regard. The extension of such logic would lead to the elimination of most subjects in the traditional arts and sciences–literature, history, foreign language, science, social sciences–because most business managers do not regularly need such knowledge in order to manage.
3. Consider an example of "non-market" community norms governing the classroom during a course I taught to MBA students in Brno, Czech Republic, in 1997. The norm among North American students is largely individual achievement, notwithstanding some group studying and notes sharing. Even group projects suffer from the pursuit of self-interest which may appear as "free-riding". These norms may reflect the relatively competitive nature of the economy and the relatively large rewards for individual achievement. In contrast, group effort was the dominant mode of behavior in my class of MBA students in the Czech Republic. This extended beyond a simple camaraderie to include considerable student-to-student consultation during lectures (apparently students teaching each other), open collaboration during written examinations (until I intervened), and even offers to help classmates during oral examinations. Perhaps this norm reflects the relatively cooperative nature of socialist society and the relatively small reward for individual achievement that was normal during the communist years.

REFERENCES

Becker, W. E. (2000). Teaching Economics in the 21st Century. *Journal of Economic Perspectives*, (Winter), 14(1), 109-119.

Blanchard, O. J.; Froot, K. A. and Sachs, J. D. (Eds.) (1994). *The Transition in Eastern Europe, Volumes I and II*. Chicago: The University of Chicago Press.

Bloom, A. (1987). *The Closing of the American Mind*. New York: Simon and Schuster.

Bosworth, B. and Ofer, G. (1995). *Reforming Planned Economies in An Integrating World Economy*. Washington, DC: Brookings Institution.

Culpan, R. (1995). "Introduction: Transforming Enterprises in Postcommunist Countries." In R. Culpan and B. N. Kumar (Eds.) *Transformation Management in Postcommunist Countries: Organizational Requirements for a Market Economy* (pp. 1-13). Westport, CT, and London: Quorum Books.

Filer, R. K.; Hamermesh, D. S.; and Rees, A. E. (1996). *The Economics of Work and Pay*. 6th Edition. New York: Harper Collins.

Fizel, J. L. and Johnson, J. D. (1986). The Effect of Macro/Micro Sequencing on Learning and Attitudes in Principles of Economics. *Journal of Economic Education* (Spring), 87-98.

Hlavacek, J. (1992). "The Case for Privatization in Czechoslovakia and other Centrally Planned Economies." In B. S. Katz and L. Rittenberg (Eds.) *The Economic Transformation of Eastern Europe: Views from Within* (pp. 3-9). Westport, CT, and London: Praeger.

Kasperson, C. J. and Dobrzynski, M. (1995). "Training and Development for a Market Economy." In Culpan and Kumar (Eds.) (pp. 119-137).

Kerkovsky, M. (1998). Lack of Information: A General Weakness of Strategic Management in Czech Companies. Possible Solutions. In Conference Proceedings for the 6th International Conference on Business and Economic Development in Central and Eastern Europe: Implications for Economic Integration into Wider Europe (pp.343-354). Conference held at the Technical University of Brno, Czech Republic (September 2-3, 1998).

Langer, J. (1998). "The Culture of Post-Communist Societies–A Challenge for Management?" In *Conference Proceedings (Brno)* (pp. 387-396).

Lazear, E. P. (ed.) (1995). Economic Transition in Eastern Europe and Russia: Realities of Reform. Stanford: Hoover Institution Press.

Marks, D. (1998a). "Can Any Economy Be a Market Economy–And Should It Be?" In *Conference Proceedings (Brno)* (pp. 437-448).

Marks, D. (1998b). Is the University a Firm? *Tertiary Education and Management*, (December), 4(4), 245-254.

Marks, D. (2001). Transition, Privatization, and Economics as a Management Technology. *International Journal of Technology Management*, 21(5/6), 529-539.

Murray, H. (1988). Management Education and the MBA: It's Time for a Rethink. *Managerial and Decision Economics*, (Winter), Special Issue, 71-78.

Siegfried, J. J.; Bartlett R. L.; Hansen, W. L.; Kelley, A. C.; McCloskey, D. N.; and Tietenberg, T. H. (1991). The Status and Prospects of the Economics Major. *Journal of Economic Education* (Summer), 197-224.

Simon Fraser University. (1990). *Calendar 1990-91*.

Smith, A. (1937). *The Wealth of Nations*. New York: Modern Library.

Soulsby, A. (1998). "Czech Management Through the Eyes of Czech Managers: A Study of Czech Managers in Privatised Enterprises." In *Conference Proceedings (Brno)* (pp. 621-630).

Spence, M. (1973). Job Market Signaling. *Quarterly Journal of Economics*, (August), 87, 355-74.

Tesar, G. (1995). *Management Education and Training: An Eastern European Perspective*. Melbourne, FL: Krieger Publishers.

Tesar, G. (1998). "International Study Exchange Programs in the United States and Europe: Closing the Gap for Students from the Central and Eastern European Economies." In *Conference Proceedings (Brno)* (pp. 631-644).

Ullmann, A. A. (1995). TeMAFL: Teaching Management as a Foreign Language. In Culpan and Kumar (Eds.) (pp. 139-149).

University of Wisconsin-Whitewater. (1992). *Graduate Business Programs 1992-4*.

Simulating Economic Development in Transformation Economies: The Role of Free-Market Processes and Government Intervention

Hugh M. Cannon
Attila Yaprak
Irene Mokra

SUMMARY. The purpose of the game described in this paper is to help students understand the impact of various strategies of government intervention on the dynamic free-market processes stimulating economic development. The game simulates three developing economies. Within the economies, each of the students represents an independent economic entity, able to contribute labor, consume goods, and acquire wealth. The game is played in periods, with each one representing a cycle of production and consumption. In one economy, students are free to act independently, or to collaborate, to invest or save money, to innovate or produce conventional products. In the other two, their activities are constrained by "government" regulations, simulating contrasting strategies of *import substitution* and *export promotion*. In the end, students are evaluated according

Hugh M. Cannon is Adcraft/Simons-Michelson Professor (E-mail: HughCannon @aol.com), Attila Yaprak is Professor and Director of the Center for International Business Studies (E-mail: Attila.Yaprak@wayne.edu), Irene Mokra is Doctoral Student in Economics (E-mail: i.mokra@wayne.edu), all at School of Business Administration, Wayne State University, 5201 Cass Avenue, Suite 300, Detroit, MI 48334-4621.

[Haworth co-indexing entry note]: "Simulating Economic Development in Transformation Economies: The Role of Free-Market Processes and Government Intervention." Cannon, Hugh M., Attila Yaprak, and Irene Mokra. Co-published simultaneously in *Journal of Teaching in International Business* (International Business Press, an imprint of The Haworth Press, Inc.) Vol. 13, No. 3/4, 2002, pp. 23-39; and: *International Business Teaching in Eastern and Central European Countries* (ed: George Tesar) International Business Press, an imprint of The Haworth Press, Inc., 2002, pp. 23-39. Single or multiple copies of this article are available for a fee from The Haworth Document Delivery Service [1-800-HAWORTH 9:00 a.m. - 5:00 p.m. (EST). E-mail address: getinfo@haworthpressinc.com].

23

to the wealth they create. The three simulated economies provide experiential evidence as a basis for discussing the relative merits of unfettered free enterprise, import substitution, and export promotion as contrasting strategies of economic development. *[Article copies available for a fee from The Haworth Document Delivery Service: 1-800-HAWORTH. E-mail address: <getinfo@haworthpressinc.com> Website: <http://www.HaworthPress.com> © 2002 by The Haworth Press, Inc. All rights reserved.]*

KEYWORDS. Simulation, stimulating economic development, import substitution, export promotion

INTRODUCTION

In a recent paper Cannon, Yaprak and Mokra (1999) developed a simulation designed to help students appreciate how the theory of free-market economics might help countries develop naturally, if left to natural market forces. This paper adds to that simulation the effects of the key governmental intervention strategies of *import substitution* and *export promotion.*

Left to its own devices, a free-market economic system depends on the self-interest of the population, perfect information, a large number of buyers and sellers, and an absence of externalities in order to promote optimal economic development. In fact, none of these conditions tend to exist in real world economies. This, in turn, provides a rationale for government intervention.

The question is whether the cure is worse than the disease. While government interventions can solve specific, targeted problems, they typically have damaging side effects as well. Indeed, government interventions can subvert many of the natural market mechanisms that stimulate growth and economic efficiency in a free-market economy. For instance, protective tariffs can shield fledgling domestic companies from the predatory practices of large foreign competitors, thus increasing the number of domestic competitors in the marketplace. But the real effect is often just the opposite. While there are more physical competitors in the domestic industry, the process removes the incentive for efficient production that exists when global competitors have direct access to the market. This represents a typical *import substitution* approach.

An alternative approach might be to provide government support for companies that are trying to become globally competitive. The cause is the same, to increase the number of competitors. This alternative also provides an incentive to create more efficient production. The problem, however, is that it provides an unfair advantage to firms who engage in export marketing over others who might strategically choose to focus on the domestic market. In effect, this distorts the natural mechanism by which the market system allocates resources to the most customer-responsive firms, focusing their attention on government policy rather than on market demand.

While the approach avoids some of the pitfalls, the *export promotion* alternative might create social norms and expectations that lead customers away from self-interest. However, not all interventions are equal. In the case of programs designed to stimulate economic growth, *import substitution and export promotion* represent dramatic contrasts in approach.

Unfortunately, the effects of the various strategies are hard to observe. The principles are abstract. The actual effects on an economy are both broad and typically contaminated by a host of other potential factors. So, how do we teach them to students? The game described in this paper creates a concrete application that is focused in both time and scope, thus making the principles easier to observe. This, in turn, provides grist for a much richer discussion of the underlying principles.

From a pedagogical perspective, the advisability, and if advisable, the type of government intervention provides an important topic for discussion. However, the principles are abstract and difficult for students to understand. We have mentioned the simulation developed by Cannon, Yaprak and Mokra (1999) to help students appreciate how the theory of free-market addresses economic development. This paper suggests modifications to the game that will help students understand and appreciate the impact of government interventions in support of economic development. It begins with a review of the underlying theory behind the free-enterprise model, and the strategies of *import substitution and export promotion*. It then reviews the PROGRESS game, as suggested by Cannon, Yaprak and Mokra (1999). Then, it proposes the changes designed to simulate the *import substitution and export promotion* approaches to economic development.

The Free-Enterprise Model

As we noted earlier, the basis of the free-enterprise system depends on the validity of four basic assumptions: *self-interest, perfect informa-*

tion, many buyers and sellers and *absence of externalities.* Exhibit 1 summarizes the theory of how the developmental process works.

In this discussion, we will speak of "people" rather than customers or companies. This reflects the notion that economic theory ultimately applies to individuals, a fact that is reflected in the fact that the *Progress* game consists of the interaction among individual students. They market the product of their labor, just as companies do. They also purchase on the same basis.

In Exhibit 1, then, demand consists of people who are willing and able to purchase need-meeting products and services (Box A). Their willingness depends on their belief that the purchase will be in their self-interest (Box B), given alternatives available (Box C), and their knowledge of the alternatives (Box D). Their ability to purchase depends on their buying power, which, in turn, depends on the degree to which they have been successful in the marketplace (Arrow E).

Notice how supply interacts with demand. Supply depends on marketing success (Arrow E), and marketing success depends on the economic rewards resulting from people's purchase decisions (Arrow F). In order to achieve these rewards, people anticipate the factors that are likely to drive market response (Arrow I). These use them to organize value-producing marketing activities (Box G), ultimately expressed in market offerings (Arrow H). These are supported by promotional efforts (Arrow J) designed to enhance the attractiveness of these offerings by stimulating people's self-interest, enhancing their knowledge of the

EXHIBIT 1. An Underlying Model of Free-Market Dynamics

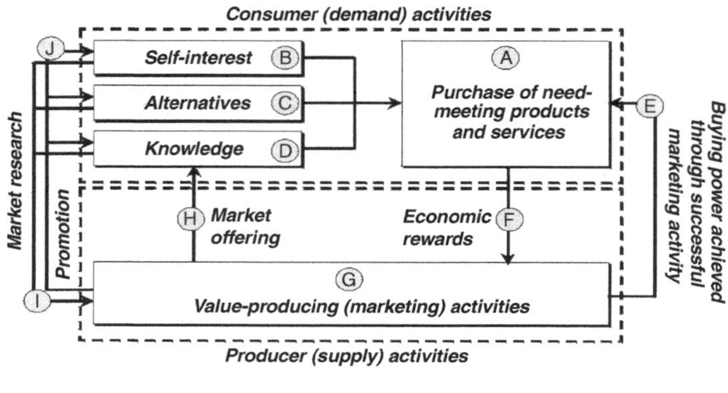

alternatives, and/or creating imagery that enhances the nature of the offerings themselves.

The more value people produce, the greater the rewards they will receive. The greater the rewards they receive, the more buying power they have, and hence, the more potential they have for meeting their own needs in the marketplace. This, of course, is nothing more than the operation of Adam Smith's classic "invisible hand," where the combined self-interest of buyers and sellers acts in concert to maximize societal satisfaction. Self-interest leads people to want more need-satisfying buying power. The way to get this is to address the needs of others. Having obtained the buying power through addressing the needs of others, others will be more attentive to one's needs. And so the process cycles, systematically focusing marketing effort where it will produce the greatest effect. The cycle is what stimulates economic growth. The more need-meeting goods and services people produce, the greater the wealth of society. The greater the wealth, the greater the stimulus for creating new need-meeting marketing innovations.

The PROGRESS game simulates this process by allowing players to use or sell labor and products in an effort to create wealth, and ultimately, create satisfaction through the consumption of products.

PROGRESS: THE FREE-ENTERPRISE GAME[1]

The game is played in a series of periods, each representing a cycle of production and consumption. In order to distinguish between satisfaction and wealth, satisfaction will be measured in *sats*. Wealth will be measured in money, or *credits*. The two are interchangeable in the sense that a player can use *credits* to buy products, which can then be consumed to acquire *sats*. However, *credits* have no intrinsic value. That is, players are not rewarded for acquiring *credits*, just *sats*. Conversely, *sats* only have intrinsic value. While they are the measure of success in the game, they cannot be spent, invested or transferred to another player.

The actual play of the game consists of a series of transactions. The vehicle through which these are recorded is the *transaction log*. Exhibit 2 provides a sample log for a hypothetical player, N01. The log illustrates how the game is played.

1. *Maintaining the Transaction Log. The basic organizational tool is each player's transaction log (Exhibit 1). The log records all transac-*

EXHIBIT 2. Sample Transaction Log for Player N01

Period	Partner Exchange	Machines Change	Machines Balance	Labor Change	Labor Balance	Product Change	A	B	C	D	E	Credits Change	Credits Balance	Sats Change	Sats Balance
1					1		0	0	0	0	0				
1	N15			+1	2		0	0	0	0	0	−15	(15)		
1	N21			+1	3		0	0	0	0	0	−15	(30)		
1	N23			+1	4		0	0	0	0	0	−20	(50)		
1	Prod			−4	0	+A16	16	0	0	0	0		0		
1	N02				0	−A10	6	0	0	0	0	+120	70		
1	Bank					−A05	1					+50	125		
1	Cons				0	−A01	0	0	0	0	0			+10	10
2	New			+1	1								125		
2	Mach	+1	1									−150	(25)		
2	N15		1	+2	3		0	0	0	0	0	−20	(45)		
2	N21		1	+1	4		0	0	0	0	0	−20	(65)		
2	N23		1	+1	5		0	0	0	0	0	−20	(85)		
2	Prod		1	−5	0	+A20	20	0	0	0	0				
2	N02		1		0	−A15	5	0	0	0	0	+195	110		
2	N02		1		0	+B01	5	1	0	0	0	−20	90		
2	N02		1		0	+C01	5	1	1	0	0	−20	70		
2	N05		1		0	+D02	5	1	1	1	0	−20	50		
2	N05		1		0	+E02	5	1	1	1	1	−20	30		
	N05		1		0	−A04	4	1	1	1	1	+40	70		
2	Cons		1		0		0	0	0	0	0		70	+70	80
3			1	+1	1								70		80

tions, ONE PER LINE. Specifically, the log includes the following information:

- *Per* refers to the *period* in which the transaction takes place.
- *Exchange Partner* refers to the *player* (if any) with whom the transaction takes place. (Note that all players will have a name: N01, N02, N03, etc.). In the example, during period 1, player N1 engaged in transactions with players N15, N21, N23, and N02.

The *log* also shows "new" to signal a new period, "prod" (exchange of labor for production), "cons" (exchange of products for *sats*), "bank" (redemption of products for *credits*), and "mach" (exchange of *credits* for a machine).

- *Machines* enable a player to increase the efficiency of a unit of labor. Each machine costs 150 credits and doubles the effectiveness of exactly one unit of labor each period. For instance, owning a machine at the beginning of a period means that the player begins with two rather than one unit of labor. In Exhibit 1, Player N01 purchased a machine at the beginning of period 2, thus increasing the value of the labor purchased from Player N15 from 1 to 2 units. If a player has more machines than labor, more than one machine can be associated with each labor unit. Two machines make one unit of labor the equivalent of three, three the equivalent of four, and so forth.
- *Labor* refers to the *balance* of available *labor* and (if this is a *labor* transaction) the amount of *labor* used or received. In the example, player N1 purchased labor from players N15, N21, and N23.
- *Product* refers to the *balance* of available *products* (A, B, C, D and E) and (if the transaction involves *products*) the amount used or received. In the example, player N01 uses its four units of labor to produce 16 units of Product A. The amount of product that can be produced with four units of labor is shown in Exhibit 3.
- *Credits* refer to the *balance* of available *credits* (money) and (if the transaction involves *credits*) the amount used or received. In the example shown in Exhibit 3, player N01 purchases labor from players N15, N21, and N23 for 15 *credits* for the first two units, and 20 *credits* the last, in period 1. She sells the 15 units of Product A for 5 *credits* each, or a total of 75 *credits*.

2. *Creating Labor. All players will receive one unit of labor each period, which they may use or sell. IT MAY NOT BE STORED. If not used*

EXHIBIT 3. Production Volume for Different Levels of Labor Input

Labor	Production*
1	1
2	4
3	9
4	16
5	20

Labor	Production
6	23
7	25
8	26
9	27
10	28

*These economies of scale only apply to production of multiple units of the same type of product (e.g. two units of labor can produce four units of A or four units of B, but not one unit of A and one unit of B).

in the period received, it will have no residual value. To sell it, they must enter it in a transaction log for both buyer and seller, along with the corresponding transfer of credits. To use it for production, the use and resulting products should be indicated in the transaction log.

3. *Creating Credits. Players have an unlimited line of bank credit. That is, they may borrow any amount they wish to finance their operations, providing they pay off their loans by the end of any period. They may pay off their loans with credits received from other players, or they may create money by exchanging products for credits. The exchange rate is fixed at 10 credits per unit, regardless of its type (A, B, C, D, or E). Players may exchange as many units as they wish at this rate.*

4. *Consuming Products. Consuming products is how players create utility, or satisfaction (sats). Exhibit 4 shows the sats consumers derive from consuming different kinds of products. Note that consuming multiple units of the same kind of product yields lower utility than a variety of products. This creates an opportunity for marketers to create value through the development of product assortments.*

5. *Determining the number of period of play. Theoretically, the game could continue indefinitely. In practice, it will be limited by the setting in which it is used. For instance, in a typical 15-week semester, the game might continue for 10 rounds. This would provide time in the beginning of the class to introduce the game, perhaps with a period in which to practice. It would also provide a period to debrief, once the game is finished.*

6. *"Winning" the Game. There are no "winners" and "losers" in the game in the competitive sense. This is critical to the concept. All the players seek to maximize their personal satisfaction, as measured by the*

EXHIBIT 4. Consumption Values

Single Type		Combination		Double Combinations		Triple Combinations		Quadruple Combinations	
Units[1]	Sats	Units[2]	Sats	Units[3*]	Sats	Units[4*]	Sats	Units[5*]	Sats
1	10	2	25	2	45	2	55	2	60
2	15	3	40	3	70	3	85	3	93
3	18	4	55	4	95	4	115	4	125
4	20	5	70	5	120	5	145	5	158

[1]Units refer to multiple units of the same product.

[2]Units refer to combinations of different products (e.g. A+B, A+B+C, etc.).

[3]Units refer to pairs of the combinations shown in the chart to the left of this one.

[4]Units refer to three of the combinations shown in the chart to the left of this one.

[5]Units refer to four of the combinations shown in the chart to the left of this one.

total number of sats acquired. This is not a "zero-sum" game. Indeed, when players act competitively, in the "zero-sum" sense of the word, everybody tends to do more poorly. The notion of a non-zero-sum game is critical to student learning, because a "zero-sum" mentality is one of the major barriers to economic development.

From a very practical perspective, the best way to manage "winning" is to evaluate players on the way they play rather than the actual results. The game administrator can often evaluate the quality of play by reviewing the actual decisions once the game is over.

The administrator can evaluate the overall results of the game by comparing it to performance norms developed over a number of games. Because they are potentially sensitive to the number of students playing the game, game administrators should take care to record the actual conditions under which each game is played.

Simulating the Effects of Government Intervention

Simulating the effects of government intervention in the PROGRESS game is as simple as establishing governments and giving them power to tax and create legislation. In order to simulate the effect of *import substitution* and *export trade promotion*, we recommend creating three "countries"–one to represent an unregulated "free-market" system, one to represent a society *using import substitution*, and one to represent a society *using export trade promotion*.

Creating a "Developed Economy"

As a rule, *export trade promotion*, and particularly *import substitution*, are used as policies designed to help developing countries progress. In order to simulate this effect, the exercise should start with a single country, *Freedonia*. One way to do this is to play the initial phase of the game in three-person teams. Then, once *Freedonia* has had time to develop, the second two "countries," *Isolationia* and *Exportonia*, can be created by taking two of the people from each *Freedonia* teams.

A Policy of Import Substitution

After creating the *import substitution* "country," *Isolationia*, the game administrator must establish a player or players to form the government. The government is free to establish any laws or regulations it deems necessary to implement a policy of *import substitution*. In order to ensure a maximum effort for success, government performance in the game will be measured by the relative success of the economy, as measured by growth in the total number of *sats* generated by the economy by the end of the game.

The only guideline the government has beyond the mandate to grow the economy is to implement a policy of *import substitution*. The instructions are as follows:

> Your task will be to stimulate growth in your newly independent country of Isolationia. To do this, you have chosen to implement a policy of *import substitution*. That is, you will seek to encourage people in your country to buy from domestic suppliers, thus strengthening the local economy and creating firms that are strong enough to compete effectively in the global market. There are no established procedures for doing this. You are free to tax, to create laws, or to otherwise manage the activities of participants in your economy as you see fit in order to implement this strategy. People within your country are also free to engage in trade with other countries, as long as the overall government policy is to encourage people to "buy domestic."

As is the case with the original PROGRESS game, there are no "winners" in the competitive sense. Rather, the game should illustrate how business success is not a zero-sum game. However, the whole purpose of the exercise is to provide a basis for discussing the relative merits of *free-market* versus *import-substitution* and *export-trade-promotion* economies. As with individual players in the game, successful trade among the "countries" is also a non-zero-sum game. However, the relative success of each of the three strategies can be seen in the growth of *sats*. This implies a comparison, and hence, the possibility of competition. Competition is natural. But the focus of the game should be on absolute success, not on "beating the competition" (the other countries).

Of course, if competition occurs between countries–as it probably will–it parallels the kind of misguided nationalism we find in the real world. This will provide a good opportunity to enrich the debriefing process by discussing the role of nationalism in the process of economic development.

A Policy of Export Trade Promotion

Instructions for the *export trade promotion* government are similar to those for import substitution. After establishing the new "country," the game administrator must establish a player or players to form the government. Again, the government is free to establish any laws or regulations it deems necessary to implement its established policy, in this case, *export trade promotion*. Again, government performance in the game will be measured by the relative success of the economy.

The guidelines for the *export-trade promotion* government are as follows:

> Your task will be to stimulate growth in your newly independent country of Exportonia. To do this, you have chosen to implement a policy of *export trade promotion*. That is, you will seek to encourage people in your country to engage in export trade, thus creating an inflow of external funds to help your country develop. There are no established procedures for doing this. You are free to tax, to create laws, or to otherwise manage the activities of participants in your economy as you see fit in order to implement this strategy. People in your country are free to engage in trade with other people inside your country, as long as the overall government policy is to encourage people to engage in export trade.

As with the case of *Isolationia*, *Exportonia's* success should not come at the expense of the other countries. Economic growth is a non-zero-sum game. The relative success of *Freedonia's* economy should reflect the superiority of *export trade promotion* over *import substitution*, not the success of the players who simulate the two governments. However, regardless of the approach the players actually take, the results should provide useful grist for discussion.

DISCUSSION

Central to the discussion of this exercise is the fact that the underlying assumptions behind the free-enterprise system might fail on all fronts. The failings may be seen as a basis for government intervention. This provides a good framework for evaluating the strategies of *import substitution* and *export trade promotion*. Both of the strategies tend to be aimed at the problem–or symptom–of underdevelopment, not its underlying causes. The debriefing process provides a good opportunity to evaluate the two strategies against a more rigorous economic framework. If the underlying assumptions of the free-enterprise system fail, what might be done to correct them?

Failures in Self-Interest

The assumption of self-interest maintains that, given adequate information and the availability of meaningful alternatives, people will make decisions that will maximize their personal satisfaction. This does not preclude working for the satisfaction of others. Indeed, one of the defining characteristics of humans is their ability to gain personal satisfaction from helping others, even at considerable personal cost or discomfort. However, self-interest does preclude making self-destructive decisions, such as unhealthy living and failure to save or otherwise plan for future problems.

A moment's reflection suggests that we are all irrational, according to this definition. We overeat, fail to exercise, spend now at the expense of long-term investment or retirement planning, neglect social relationships that offer potential for great long-term satisfaction, and so forth. Indeed, these are behaviors that invalidate the free-enterprise model. For instance, if people fail to care for their health when young, and fail to save for medical expenses when old, they will suffer, and society will not maximize its satisfaction.

Cannon and Yaprak (1997) support this intuitive argument. They argue that irrationality not only exists, but that a careful study of the way people make decisions would lead us to expect it. The central concept is that people tend to be governed by what March and Simon (1958) refer to as "bounded rationality." Natural limitations in the way people process information limit them to considering a relatively few alternatives and evaluative criteria at a time. They are "rational" in the way they consider these alternatives, but "irrational" in that many attractive alternatives and criteria simply do not get considered.

Exhibit 5 describes the process. It suggests that people develop a kind of psychological *action plan* (Box C) to govern their thinking in a given situation. The selection of the plan depends on both the demands of the situation (Box A) and the personal needs of the individual (Box B). The bias toward short-term thinking is not inevitable, but likely, since a key factor in defining a situation is short-term need arousal (Box A). Similarly, situational needs and norms tend to address immediate problems, not necessarily long-term welfare.

EXHIBIT 5. A Theory of Economic Irrationality

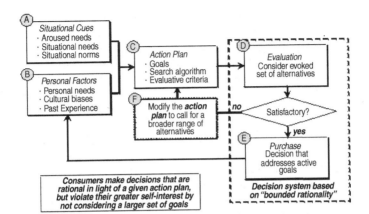

Box B reflects the role of personal factors, as reflected through personal needs, cultural biases and past experience. Given the uncertainties of life, people develop behavioral rules of thumb based on what they see around them. For instance, a person whose needs are typically not met will tend to have personal experiences that are shaped by a focus on short-term problem-solving, generally at the expense of long-term planning. When most people share the same deprivation, their collective experience tends to shape a culture that focuses on short-term thinking. We see this in many developing countries, where people seem ready to sacrifice the potential for long-term prosperity in return for a bribe or other personal benefit that is socially destructive.

Of course, long-term social destruction is also destructive to the lifestyles of the individuals living within the society.

The *action plan* (Box C) governs the goals people seek to pursue in any given situation, along with the search algorithm through which they seek to identify alternatives. It also determines the criteria by which consumers evaluate the alternatives.

Box D represents the actual problem solving process. People evaluate the alternatives, using the selected action plan, as long as this seems to work (Box E). If it doesn't work, they seek to modify the plan so that it does (Box F).

The key to the process seems to be situational and personal factors. While these can be influenced by experience, the process is a slow one. Bad habits persist for a long time, both individually and collectively.

The implications are that society might want to offset or mold their effects by utilizing the tools suggested in Boxes A and B. For instance, education provides a good intervention. People can learn that effective business decisions require long-term thinking ("situational needs" in Box A). Similarly, they can learn that long-term thinking is one of the things good executives should do ("situational norms" in Box A). Case histories can be used to show that long-term thinking is generally a good way to get what you want ("personal needs" in Box B), generating a kind of vicarious experience to support this connection ("past experience" in Box B). The long-term effect of these efforts can actually shift the way people tend to look at business problems ("cultural biases" in Box B).

These kinds of interventions might be framed as a type of *export trade promotion*, but not as *import substitution*. Furthermore the focus on export, as opposed to domestic, trade is purely a matter of convenience. Where foreign countries experience a higher level of economic development, they are likely to provide lucrative markets, and attractive sources of modern technology. However, the whole purpose of the PROGRESS game is to illustrate how wealth is created, even in the absence of a prosperous national trading partner.

Failures of Perfect Information

Perhaps the most obvious failing of any economy is in the lack of information available to decision makers. This involves everything from a lack of information regarding who is providing what kinds of products and services to a knowledge of what customers need and how they will respond to a particular market offering.

This provides another natural place for government intervention. In the real world, information services, infrastructure investment in the Internet, and so forth all constitute forms of investment in improved market information.

In the game, the "government" players will probably discover the need for information – most obviously, information about who has what to sell at what price, but also information regarding future possibilities and trends, the strategic positions of various companies, and so forth. Of course, the information has value for the players, and hence, their self-interest should drive them to pay for it. However, as we have seen, short-term thinking, lack of experience, and cultural biases can all mitigate against the spontaneous investment in information. This is true in the game, as well. As Exhibit 5 suggests, players will likely engage in a kind of "satisfying" behavior, engaging in transactions that are convenient and consistent with their cultural norms, rather than maximizing their utility. For instance, experience in the PROGRESS game suggests that players will often seek to be "managers" rather than selling their labor, even when the economics of the situation make selling labor more attractive. They will likely stick with established sales and supply relationships, as long as they are satisfactory, rather than seeking to optimize the system.

One of the things a government might do is take actions that will increase the amount of information available to the students playing the game. In the debriefing session, discussing the role of information and how it was or was not used will be very important in helping students understand the lessons of economic growth. More important will be a discussion of the various means by which information can be delivered to the marketplace. Theory would suggest that the best way would be to market it, so that companies come to recognize its value and begin to demand it.

Failures in the Number of Buyers and Sellers

Both the PROGRESS game and this governmental modification begin with each player acting as both a buyer and seller. There are, however, significant economies of scale available to drive players to combine their efforts. Economies of scale that motivate coordinated activity can also lead to unhealthy constraints of trade. Indeed, one of the economic arguments people provide in support of *import substitution* is the need to foster new domestic business development by protecting it from predatory global competition.

In the game, issues of monopoly will rarely be raised in the natural course of play. However, in debriefing, the issues can play a prominent role in understanding what has really happened. For instance, notwithstanding the theoretical rationale for *import substitution*, the effect is generally to decrease the competition, giving domestic firms monopolistic, or at least oligopolistic, powers. As the game continues, and the companies grow and mature, the larger companies provide an opportunity to discuss how modern forms of joint-venture management and unbundling of services can provide economies of scale without creating monopolistic structures.

The Problem of Externalities

Externalities consist of situations where the decisions of one economic unit affect the welfare of another who has not participated in the decision. When these situations occur, they provide a justification for government involvement to counteract the effects of the externality. For instance, if someone invests in the development of Internet technology, and the economy grows as a result, everyone benefits, whether or not they use the Internet. This, then, suggests that they should bear part of the expense.

This is the rationale provided for getting government involved in the business of economic development. If everyone in the society benefits, they should all participate (through their tax money and the activities of their governmental representatives). If we argue that any failure in the fundamental economic assumptions behind the free-enterprise system hurts everyone in a society, this provides a rationale for government becoming involved in addressing these failures. This argument should play a prominent role in the discussion of the game.

SUMMARY AND CONCLUSIONS

In the initial presentation of the PROGRESS game, Cannon, Yaprak and Mokra (1999) suggested that one of its major benefits is that it can be easily modified to simulate other economic effects, one of which was a government effect. This paper addresses that possibility. It provides direct and immediate experience with the impact government activities can have on a simulated economy. While it does not simulate every possible effect, it provides the grist for some very productive discussions of what might happen in a real economy as a result of various types of government interventions. Students who have just completed the game will typically have an easy time imagining various different scenarios that would otherwise seem abstract and irrelevant.

Again, the promise of the game is to provide a laboratory for simulating a host of economic effects, only one of which is government intervention. Hopefully, the future will bring additional modifications that can be used to sensitize students to specific issues, including everything from various types of government strategy (such as the two addressed here) to social issues, such as cultural biases and issues of diversity.

Even more important, we hope the future will bring reports of actual classroom testing. The nature of a simulation is never fully understood until it has been tested in a variety of different educational and laboratory settings. PROGRESS was designed to elicit different patterns of activity with different types of students. If this was true of the basic game, it should be even truer of the type of government intervention introduced in this paper.

NOTE

1. This section is taken from Hugh M. Cannon, Attila Yaprak and Irene Mokra, "Progress: An Experiential Exercise in Developmental Marketing." *Developments in Business Simulation and Experiential Learning*, Volume 26 (1999), 265-273.

REFERENCES

Bruton, H. (1998), A Reconsideration of Import Substitution. *Journal of Economic Literature*, June, pp. 903-936.

Cannon, H. & Yaprak, A. (1997), " 'Marketing' Export Marketing: An Alternative Approach to Trade Promotion Assistance." Paper presented to the 1997 Annual Conference of the Academy of International Business, Monterrey, MX, (October).

Cannon, H. & Yaprak, A. (1998). "Marketing and Economic Development: Implications for Emerging Economies." Paper presented to the Consortium for International Marketing Research Conference on Globalization, The International Firm and Emerging Economies, Izmir, Turkey, (May).

Gentry, J. (1990). "What Is Experiential Learning?" In J. W. Gentry (ed.), *Guide to Business Gaming and Experiential Learning*. East Brunswick: Nichols/GP Publishing, pp. 9-20.

Grabowski, R. (1994). Import Substitution, Export Promotion, and the State in Economic Development. *Journal of Developing Areas*, July, pp. 535-554.

Hoover, J. (1974) "Experiential Learning: Conceptualization and Definition." In *Simulation, Games and Experiential Techniques: On the Road to a New Frontier*, James Kenderdine and Bernard Keys (eds.), pp. 31-35.

Keith, R. (1960). The Marketing Revolution. *Journal of Marketing*, January, pp. 35-38.

Kolb, D. (1984). *Experiential Learning: Experience as the Source of Learning and Development*. Englewood Cliffs, NJ: Prentice-Hall.

Kruger, A. (1985). Import Substitution Versus Export Promotion. *Finance and Development*, June, pp. 20-23.

Lewin, K. (1951). *Field Theory in the Social Sciences*. New York: Harper & Row.

Smith, W. (1956). Product Differentiation and Market Segmentation as Alternative Marketing Strategies. *Journal of Marketing*, July, pp. 3-8.

The Use of Cases
in Teaching Business Courses
in Central and Eastern Europe
and the United States

Tom Bramorski

SUMMARY. The extent of case methodology use in teaching business courses in Central and Eastern Europe (CEE) and in the United States (US) differ. This paper discusses the reasons for these differences utilizing the available literature and the author's recent experiences in teaching business courses in CEE under the Fulbright Scholar Program. It also presents a framework for developing and delivering case-based business courses with the objective of maximizing teaching effectiveness. *[Article copies available for a fee from The Haworth Document Delivery Service: 1-800-HAWORTH. E-mail address: <getinfo@haworthpressinc.com> Website: <http://www. HaworthPress.com> © 2002 by The Haworth Press, Inc. All rights reserved.]*

KEYWORDS. Central and Eastern Europe, teaching, case methodology

Tom Bramorski is Professor of Management at the University of Wisconsin-Whitewater, 800 West Main Street, Whitewater, WI 53190 (E-mail: bramorst@mail.uww.edu).

The author wishes to acknowledge the generous support of the Council for International Exchange of Scholars (CIES) for making the Fulbright experience in Poland possible.

[Haworth co-indexing entry note]: "The Use of Cases in Teaching Business Courses in Central and Eastern Europe and the United States." Bramorski, Tom. Co-published simultaneously in *Journal of Teaching in International Business* (International Business Press, an imprint of The Haworth Press, Inc.) Vol. 13, No. 3/4, 2002, pp. 41-55; and: *International Business Teaching in Eastern and Central European Countries* (ed: George Tesar) International Business Press, an imprint of The Haworth Press, Inc., 2002, pp. 41-55. Single or multiple copies of this article are available for a fee from The Haworth Document Delivery Service [1-800-HAWORTH 9:00 a.m. - 5:00 p.m. (EST). E-mail address: getinfo@haworthpressinc.com].

INTRODUCTION

Both the tempo and the scope of economic transformations occurring in CEE create demand for business management talent. However, due to multiple structural reasons and organizational inertia, traditional universities in CEE have been relatively slow to adapt to the needs of the market. Many of them continue to produce graduates possessing a narrow range of specialist technical skills while today's employers frequently search for generalists with excellent communication, information technology and people management skills. Business education institutions are expected to provide their graduates with a set of learning skills, analytical tools and evaluation methodologies. A specific task of focusing the new hires on company-relevant problems is frequently left to the internal resources of the employer (Dyker, 1997).

The process of retraining managers of privatized enterprises throughout CEE has not been a great success either. It is challenging and time consuming to change the fundamental beliefs and values developed under the old economic system. This produced a significant gap between demand and supply of individuals prepared to effectively function in the free market economy. Sensing business opportunities many private business schools have emerged. In order to create the conditions necessary to stimulate the economic growth of CEE, there is an urgent need to develop an education strategy aimed at meeting the demand for management expertise in the medium and long-range (Bozyk, 1999) and (Lungershausen, 1999).

The differences in both the methodology and content of business programs in CEE and the US are largely due to cultural differences between the regions. Business programs in the US have evolved over a time and tend to be better structured, more practical and oriented more toward enhancing student professional careers. They are also better attuned to the changing market needs compared to the programs in CEE. For example, the feedback provided to educators by members of their program industry advisory groups provides a basis for course and program changes and new program development, while in CEE such feedback is virtually nonexistent. Moreover, in US academic institutions program budgets take into account the demand for courses comprising these programs, which sometimes leads to course cancellations or program elimination. In CEE courses are rarely cancelled, while instructional and academic program support budgets are developed and allocated at the central level. This approach reduces the need for program marketing and leads to situations where program offerings do not always reflect market demand while courses and programs that have low or high demand receive the same support (Bramorski, 1998).

To some degree the differences in business education are also due to the fact that business education in CEE is in the stage of development and growth, while in the US it is in the phase of saturation. This makes the US institutions more competitive in their efforts to attract and retain students relative to their CEE counterparts. Due to a high demand for and a short supply of high quality business programs entry into these programs is highly selective in academic institutions throughout CEE while retention of students is not an issue (Bramorski, 1998). Further, the well-established academic institutions in CEE face a challenge of having to transform their business programs to better meet current market needs. This involves developing new programs and retraining faculty and providing appropriate infrastructure and marketing support. Such major transformations require appropriate allocation of resources for these developments and often have to overcome significant organizational inertia.

It is important to note that a mere adoption of the education model proven to work well in one country is no guarantee of success of the same model in another. However, there are lessons to be learned from the US experiences by CEE educators and administrators. There is a strong agreement that the way to improve the effectiveness of business programs in CEE is a broad adoption of a case-oriented teaching methodology. The case model has been used in many leading US business programs for many years. Students learn from the instructor and textbooks/lecture notes, which is the traditional learning mode, and also from other sources. These sources include student group members, business executives invited to lectures, traditional and modern library resources (specifically including the electronic collections), the Internet, international exchange programs, business internships with credit applied toward degree requirements, etc. These approaches enhance the quality of course presentations and develop networking opportunities for participating students and faculty.

Using cases allows the instructor and the students to bring a real company to the classroom and simulate its performance. As evidenced by the experiences of business schools in the US, the case approach with appropriate infrastructural support will improve overall teaching effectiveness in terms of the subject matter as well as the diagnostic and analytical skills, interpersonal and communication skills. Achieving the goal of improving teaching effectiveness is enhanced by the adoption of Information Technology (IT) teaching support tools, including hardware for PowerPoint and multimedia presentations in classrooms, on-line testing over the Internet, Web-based course delivery in real-time and others. The use of the IT tools in the development and delivery of business courses in the US is widespread. In CEE institutions offering business programs, the use of IT is rudimentary and its availability to faculty and students is restricted (Bramorski, 1998).

The advantages of using the case method approach to instruction based on Harvard Business School applications are presented in Barnes (1994), who makes suggestions gained from experimentation with course concepts and materials. These changes include the size and composition of participant groups, multiple seminar time lengths, the impact of the architectural design of the seminar room, and the administrative protocols employed on patterns of student contribution. The use of case study discussions in the organizational communication class as an effective instructional technique is also discussed in Byers (1998), who evaluates a variety of formats such as the World Wide Web, local and national news publications, local business and industry, and self-developed case studies and discusses methods for facilitating case study discussions. The challenge of preparing students to be lifelong learners capable of facing emerging challenges lies not as much in continually changing the business curriculum, but in preparing graduates to continually change and to learn the things they need throughout life. The benefits of using cases to teach business courses to achieve the continuous change objective in students are discussed in Celuch (1999) and a comprehensive presentation of practical approaches to effectively using cases in teaching undergraduate, MBA and executive level business programs is available in Erskine (1998).

USING CASES IN TEACHING BUSINESS PROGRAMS IN THE US

Undergraduate business programs in US schools are typically four years long and lead to a Bachelors degree in Business Administration (BBA). Specific programs (e.g., accounting, finance) may offer their own degrees subject to individual university and program requirements. During the first two years future business students are required to gain general education from outside business (e.g. religion, foreign languages, and history). As using cases effectively requires exposure to functional foundation courses, the use of cases is viable in classes taken in the third and fourth years. The senior-level classes that lend themselves naturally to the use of cases to discuss cases along processes rather than along functional lines include manufacturing strategy, marketing strategy, advanced finance, and administrative policy. It is important to note that fourth year students have the knowledge from prerequisite courses as well as from other experiences, including internships in industry or participation in international exchanges. This combination of knowledge and experience can be effectively applied to identify and analyze business process problems using the case methodology.

Two-year graduate business programs leading to a general MBA or functional MS degrees typically restrict admission based on prior relevant business experience. Therefore, graduate business students are expected to be able to better link theory and practice compared to undergraduate students who typically lack relevant business experience. Graduate students work in groups that analyze a selected real business problem that they themselves identify. A typical result of this analysis is a written team research paper that is presented to the class and the participating company. Outstanding student papers are frequently submitted to professional academic and professional conferences, journals and paper competitions. An approach to effectively use cases in teaching undergraduate and graduate courses in accounting and finance is discussed in Mohrman (1999). The method focuses on the integration of basic theoretical concepts with practice in the classroom through the use of current accounting and financial articles. The results indicate that this approach significantly enhances the level of student understanding of the subject matter. A framework for researching and analyzing applied cases in business classes is shown in Figure 1.

Many of the recent approaches in business college instruction emphasize active learning by students (collaborative learning) as opposed to traditional instruction. Practical problem-centered (case) instruction is one type of collaborative learning. Since cases are learner-based and action-oriented, students gain experience in analysis, creativity, decision making, and in accepting responsibility for future consequences. The benefits of problem-centered instruction are presented in Thomchick (1997) and Cuseo (1994).

The foundation of the educational philosophy and practice of the many US business colleges is the recognition of the distinction between the younger college student and the student who has assumed the adult responsibilities of self-determination, financial independence, and professional development. Traditionally, the role of the student in a classroom has been relatively passive. However, the educational case-ori-

FIGURE 1. A Framework for Analyzing Business Problems Using Cases

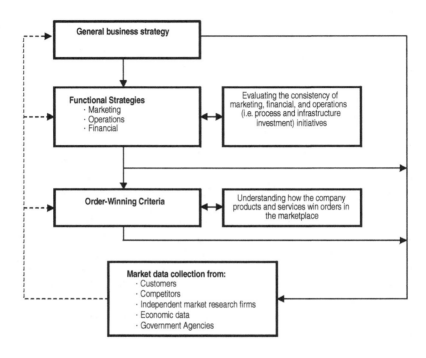

ented model demands active participation by students in their educational process, thus placing substantial responsibility on the learner. There are four critical learning objectives in using the case methodology to teaching business courses.

The first of these is shared participant responsibility for self-directed learning and small group learning dynamics. Professional and personal growths require that individuals develop the skills necessary to manage their own learning. The participants are expected to seek answers to their questions, identify and develop resources for their concerns, and take charge of their own learning. For this reason the programs using study groups and cases have been designed to provide the structure and support necessary to encourage independence and self-direction.

The second objective is to develop the interpersonal skills necessary for effective participation in the workings of groups. Study groups are an integrated part of the educational model consistent with the case analysis requirements. The groups, comprised of two to five students each, meet regularly outside of class and function as mutual support mechanisms through which students can learn more efficient problem solving from the professional expertise of peers. In this model, students and instructors are major learning sources and that individuals learn from one another by participation in the process of inquiry and involvement with the study group consistent with the concept of shared learning responsibility. Typically, US students enthusiastically support the use of study groups as a tool particularly in situations involving the analysis of business cases. Exit surveys of business school graduates consistently indicate that the study group concept is extremely beneficial in helping students achieve the prescribed learning outcomes. When students accept the fact that they can learn from one another, a system of trust and support evolves and the learning process becomes interactive.

Working adults have significantly less time to devote to full-time, formal education compared to full-time students. Through combining and sharing the talents, experience, and learning resources of the study group, adult students assume a greater self-direction and responsibility for their learning. By sharing the learning and responsibilities, more information can be disseminated among the group members within a limited amount of time. This approach covers more subject matter content than could be achieved through an individual effort. In addition, the importance of traditional instruction is diminished allowing more classroom time for presentations, Q&A sessions and discussions. The study group members make the commitment to work together and assist each other in meeting the objectives and outcomes of the course. In situations involving case analyses, the business curriculum is typically designed to focus on participative learning outcomes. Through the study group process, the learning process is enhanced, because students are provided with the opportunity to analyze their experiences and compare and contrast these experiences with theories presented in the curriculum materials.

The third objective is improving the individual's listening, writing and verbal communication skills that are essential in today's business world. As noted in the introduction, many business executives consider these "soft" skills more important that the "hard" technical skills. The reason is that the technical business skills can be taught fairly easily to an individual with the right combination of interpersonal and communication skills, while the opposite is not true. Study groups meet outside the required class time to discuss and prepare assignments and share learning resources. Each course generally requires a group project in the form of a written and/or an oral report, usually presented to the class for discussion and critique. Group grades are awarded (jointly by the instructor and by other group members), so the ability to integrate and evaluate each member's total participation in the tasks of the group becomes the responsibility of all group members rather than the instructor alone. A compound evaluation score will be reflected in the final grade at the end of the course.

The fourth objective is improving the individual's ability to utilize modern information technology–a skill that is necessary in today's business world. In order to achieve this objective, students are required to use tools such as PowerPoint and the Internet to communicate and to prepare and deliver their presentations and written case analyses. This ability is particularly relevant for increasingly popular Web delivery format used by many institutions in teaching business courses. Notably, Web instruction technologies have opened up access to Masters level business degree programs to the working professionals. These students are either unable or unwilling to interrupt their professional careers in order to complete their degree in a traditional campus environment. The Web-based business programs award them an opportunity to complete the degree requirements while working. In the electronic environment communication, verbal and written presentations and research processes are completed without students even having to ever come to the traditional campus. The experiences with distance learning at Siemens Business Communications Systems are presented in Wilson (1998). The author concludes that the Virtual University is more conducive to learning because courses are structured in bite-size modules, homework involves tasks in real-work settings and students return for follow-up sessions. However, Web-based training is found to be unsuitable for teaching behavioral skills because that usually requires role-playing.

In order to achieve the case learning objectives presented above classes are typically divided into student study groups consisting of two to five students. The groups select a current and practical case to analyze. Each study group should prepare a written report with their analysis of the problems and recommendations, which should be presented to the entire class and discussed. Discussion and interaction between the students in study groups is a major component of the case-oriented learning format. This is particularly useful for adult students who have more real-world related experience that they can share with their groups compared to traditional on-campus students. Therefore, every student's active participation in the works of study groups and in the classroom is a critical element of learning. This applies particularly to the material that needs to be evaluated from the practitioner's perspective as well as the more theoretical material presented by the instructor. Some suggestions to instructors regarding the use of case methodology for teaching business courses are quoted below after (Bramorski, 1999).

- The student study groups will typically be able to identify good real-world business applications for these reports based on their own experiences. Rarely should the instructor suggest a current topic based solely on his/her knowledge and experience. This step is easily accomplished in the traditional as well as the Web-based course settings.
- The instructor should overview the particulars regarding the format and content of the written group reports. Typically, the reports are be prepared on a computer using a standard writing style and format and should not be longer than 20 pages including all references, tables, charts, etc. This step is also easily accomplished in all course settings.
- In-progress reports should be prepared and submitted by the student groups at various times throughout the course. The purpose is to ensure that students start the work early and work consistently throughout the course duration. These reports may be in the form of asynchronous communications such as e-mail exchanges or electronic real-time discussions groups under Microsoft NetMeeting or other communication programs.
- The instructor should allow approximately 20 minutes for the oral presentation and discussion of each study group report in the classroom. Student groups should be advised to rehearse your presentation to make it interesting and to the point. The detailed analysis of the business problem should be included in the written report. The purpose of the oral presentation is to make the audience want to look into the written report for these details. This step is suitable for the traditional setting but it is hard to implement in the Web-based setting. Even though electronic presentation in real time is technically possible, existing communications network and PC workstation speed and throughput limitations frequently make real-time and high quality electronic interactions difficult. If such technical limitations exist, presentations pre-recorded on a CD and other student assignments can be delivered via conventional means. Communications between the student and the instructor will then be limited to the asynchronous mode.

USING CASES IN TEACHING BUSINESS PROGRAMS IN CEE

Capitalizing on a growing need for business education, many educational institutions in CEE have developed business education programs that widely vary in terms of content, environment and delivery quality. Some leading programs are accredited nationally or internationally, have numerous international linkages with academic institutions in Europe and North America and impose strict requirements on who is eligible to teach these courses. Some technical programs opted to achieve ISO-9000 certification. Many business programs, however, continue to lack instructors who are capable of discussing problems across narrow functional silos and qualified to teach case-oriented business courses by establishing relevant publications portfolios and/or graduating from a reputable PhD degree-granting business program (Bramorski, 1998) and (Przybylowski, 1998).

Another challenging issue is the ability of educational institutions to attract and retain instructors able to effectively merge theory and practice. The problem is compounded by the fact that salaries of business educators throughout CEE institutions are generally not competitive forcing many talented individuals out of the field. Those who stay in teaching are often compelled to hold multiple assignments at different academic institutions frequently located at different academic centers. This makes it difficult to focus on identifying long-term educational needs leading to systematic curricular developments and complementary research and consulting activities necessary for effective case teaching (Bramorski, 1998).

The final organizational factor affecting the development and deployment of the case teaching model in business throughout CEE is unwillingness of the senior educational cadres and administrators in many CEE business education institutions to adopt their skills to transformed market needs. This is demonstrated by a relative lack of focus of many existing business degree programs in which courses developing skills and knowledge in areas such as managing quality, projects, people and information technology are mixed with (frequently not current) traditional offerings. The problem is further exacerbated by the universal use in CEE of traditional promotion standards that rarely take into account factors such as course content, popularity with students and instructor rankings. Hence, changing the organizational cultures as well as producing and retaining faculties with appropriate teaching credentials, research record and practical experience should be viewed as one of the top priorities of educational executives and administrators throughout CEE.

Strong demand for business programs throughout CEE combined with a relatively low supply of quality programs allows business programs to become highly selective. Recognizing that high quality of education is in part determined by the knowledge and experience of their students, these institutions carefully screen their perspective students. However, many business programs do not impose such requirements on the credentials of their instructors. This leads, for example, to foreign instructors with background in non-business fields conducting specialized business classes in a foreign language. The sole benefit to a local participant of such programs is in the exposure to the foreign language and the business terminology. Since many programs throughout CEE are becoming merely professional certificate programs, developing and implementing a comprehensive business education strategy based on a case teaching model is difficult (Bramorski, 1998).

The use of cases in teaching business at CEE business schools is relatively infrequent compared to the US despite the fact that there are many businesses in CEE that could provide an excellent teaching material. This is, in part, due to the fact that for competitive reasons, the businesses in CEE withhold information that is publicly available to potential investors and academics in the US. Significant case development work needs to be done to create case libraries documenting the practices of local businesses and then to formally incorporate these cases as a teaching tool in senior level business classes. These two goals can be achieved by utilizing substantial accomplishments of US business schools in this area. For example, Harvard Business School has opened an office in Silicon Valley in 1998 to develop case studies for teaching classes about Internet company startups. Sloan School of Management at MIT decided to accommodate growing student interest in the Internet by offering a new track of courses in electronic commerce and on-line marketing. It also plans to expand a separate Entrepreneurship Center to create and sustain local technology companies. Similar efforts are under way at Vanderbilt University, Carnegie Mellon and other leading business schools. The need to support the case-based instruction methodology throughout North American business colleges has led to the creation of four major business case libraries located at Harvard Business School, Darden Graduate School of Business, Ivey School of Business and the University of Denver. The Web sites of these institutions present detailed statistics regarding their case collections by business discipline. They also contain standard course descriptions of business courses that utilize the case approach. While the content of the business case databases is rapidly changing with some 500 new cases becoming available per quarter, these databases already contain over 16,000 current case studies from all business disciplines. A similar development takes place in Europe with cases needed to support teaching business courses being available on the Web through The European Case Clearing House (ECCH).

The case collections of leading North American and European universities could be used as useful resources for academic institutions in CEE considering adopting the case approach to teaching business courses to their constituents. Similarly, the experiences of these institutions could be used as useful benchmarks for evaluating teaching curricula, methodologies and effectiveness.

THE EFFECTIVENESS OF CASES
AS A TEACHING TOOL IN BUSINESS CLASSES

The issue of evaluating effectiveness in a case-based environment has attracted the attention of many researchers. Using computer facilities was shown to be helpful in demonstrating real-world applications, while poor data or inappropriate case studies might hinder the applications of the computer programs in classroom teaching (Yeong, 2000). The method of establishing standards for judging and assessing elements of critical thinking is also presented in Celuch (1999). The effectiveness of using real-life cases (available in *Money* magazine) in a personal finance or senior-level financial planning course is discussed in St. Pierre (1997). These references emphasize that the cases require group interaction the instructor leaving the room for individual problem identification and solution recommendation that the courses be and positively received by students.

In earlier sections, we discussed the major structural issues involved in teaching business courses using a case methodology. A question in this section is how to measure its effectiveness. To achieve this goal, we propose a rating-scale approach. First, a committee consisting of faculty, administrators and students select a set of issues to be covered and designs appropriate questionnaires. The committee allocates relative weights to each issue while the class participants allocate the ranking on a point scale (from 0 to 5). The sum of weights and rating products can be used as a basis to compare courses while the analysis of responses to specific questions determines areas for improvement. The evaluation factors depend on the university and some on the instructor. Selected factors that depend on the quality of *institutional support* include, but are not limited to:

- Quality of pre-delivery activities (course promotion, ease of registration, etc.)
- Quality of food and accommodations (where applicable)
- Quality of the lecture room (sufficient number and comfort of seats, lighting, heating and air conditioning, noise control, etc.)
- Quality and availability of course materials (hard and soft copies, proceedings, notes, handouts, etc.)
- Availability and quality of traditional presentation support (white boards, microphone/speakers, transparency projectors, etc.)
- Availability of multimedia support in the lecture facility (computer hookups, VCR and TV, Internet, PowerPoint support, etc.)
- Availability of information technology necessary to support course delivery and group interactions in the Web environment (high-speed Internet connections, modem-equipped notebooks, standard software platforms, etc.)
  Selected factors that depend on the *instructor* include, but are not limited to:
- Instructor knowledge of the subject matter (breadth, depth, currency, etc.)
- Instructor personality (friendliness, personal contact with the audience, etc.)
- Quality of instructor-written or instructor-selected, cases, instructional material or examples used in the course (clarity, organization, local origin of the case material, case relevance and applicability, etc.)
- The degree of participant's involvement (time available for questions, class discussion, team presentations, examples, etc.)
- Quality and availability of content-supporting activities (plant tours, guest speakers, etc.)
- Presentation speed and technique (too fast, hard to understand, sentences too long, etc.)
- Organization of the presentation (breaks, enough time to read displayed material, etc.).

As discussed in Bramorski (1999), a course may be rated high overall only when it is rated high on both instructor-related and the university-related factors. Responses to specific questions should serve as a basis for making specific course improvements. This is illustrated in Figure 2.

FIGURE 2. The Dependence of Overall Teaching Effectiveness on the Organizational and Instructor-Specific Factors

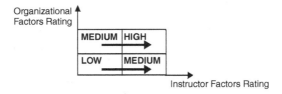

North American universities and professional associations as well as The European Case Clearing House (ECCH) offer workshops and seminars on case writing, using and evaluating teaching effectiveness in courses where the case approach is used. These experiences can be of particular value to CEE business faculty utilizing the case approach at their institutions.

CONCLUSIONS

This paper presented on the methodology of conducting business courses using a case approach. Specific issues that were enhanced by using the case approach were discussed. It was noted that using the case approach effectively requires the students to learn not only a narrow set of functional competencies but–more importantly–a variety of "soft" business skills specifically including communication skills and ability to work in teams. Overall effectiveness of the case-based method of teaching business courses was found to depend on a combination of factors related to the subject matter, the instructor and the organizational infrastructure.

REFERENCES

Barnes, L.B. (1994). *Teaching and the Case Method. Text, Cases, and Readings* (3rd ed.). Boston: Harvard Business School Press.

Berkman, K. and Bradbury, M. (1998). Instructional Case: Evergreen Forests Limited. *Issues in Accounting Education*, (November), 13 (4), 869-879.

Bozyk, P. (1999). 24 *Countries of Central and Eastern Europe. The Transformation.* Warsaw, Poland: The Main School of Economics.

Bramorski, T. (1999). "The Use of Case Methodology in Teaching Business Courses in Poland and in the United States." In A. Koziol (Ed.) *Quality for the XXIst Century* (pp. 871-879). Conference held at the Poznan University of Economics, Poznan, Poland (September 5-11).

Bramorski, T. (1998). *Professional Experiences as a Senior Fulbright Program Scholar in Central and Eastern Europe.*

Byers, P.Y. (1998). Case Studies in the Organizational Communication Course: Applying Textbook Concepts to Real Life Organizations. Paper presented at the Annual Meeting of the Central States Communication Association.

Celuch, K. and Slama, M. (1999). Teaching Critical Thinking Skills for the 21st Century: An Advertising Principles Case Study, (January-February). *Journal of Marketing Theory and Practice* 74 (3), 134-140.

Cuseo, J.B. (1994). Critical Thinking and Cooperative Learning: A Natural Marriage, in Cooperative Learning and College. *Teaching*, (Winter), 4, 2-5.

Dyker, D.A. (1997). *The Technology of Transition. Science and Technology Policies for Transition Countries*, Budapest: Central European University Press.

Erskine, J.A., Leenders, M.R. and Leenders, L. (1998). *Teaching with Cases* (Second Edition) London, Ontario, Canada: Ivey Publishing, Ivey Business School.

Lungershausen, H.(1999). International Networks of Responsible People Dedicated to Sustainable Development. In A. Koziol (Ed.) Quality for the XXIst Century (pp. 880-887). Conference held at the Poznan University of Economics, Poznan, Poland (September 5-11).

Mohrman, M.B. (1999). Instructional Case: General Host: Accounting for a Bond Refunding. *Issues in Accounting Education*, (August), 14 (3), 451-465.

Przybylowski, K., Tokarski, M., Gruin, M., Jelenikova, S., and Rudelius, W. (1998). "Management Training in Central and Eastern Europe: Shocks, Synergies, and Strategies." In K. Rais (Ed.) *Business and Economic Development in Central and Eastern Europe: Implications for Economic Integration into Wider Europe*, Brno, Czech Republic, (September 2-3), 553-559.

St. Pierre, E. (1997). Using Family Case Studies to Supplement a Financial Planning Course *Financial Practice & Education*, (Fall-Winter), 7 (2), 94-98.

Thomchick, E. (1997). The Use of Collaborative Learning in Logistics Classes. *Journal of Business Logistics*, 18 (2), 191-206.

Wilson, L. (1998). Project: Siemens Business Communications Systems, Inc.: Virtual Training Saves $800K in First Year *Computerworld* March 23.

Yeong-T.S. and Liang, C.L. (2000). Using Multivariate Rank Sum Tests to Evaluate Effectiveness of Computer Applications in Teaching Business Statistics *Journal of Applied Statistics*, (March), 27 (3), 337-346.

Collaborative Learning Instrument in Teaching Entrepreneurship Issues

Alina M. Zapalska

Geoff Perry

SUMMARY. Due to the shortcomings associated with the largely passive learning experience currently experienced by students at the University level in Central and Eastern Europe, active learning approaches have been promoted by educationalists as a more effective method for teaching business and entrepreneurship. This paper contributes to this literature by outlining a collaborative learning instrument involving active learning that can be used to teach entrepreneurship at university level in Central and Eastern Europe. This instrument illustrates the role of entrepreneurship and proprietorship in both a well-established market economy and in the post-communist economies of Central and Eastern Europe. Students outcomes should include the following: firstly, the recognition that the emerging small business sectors of the post-communist economies have much potential as a vehicle for economic growth and for developing capitalist forms of economic production; secondly, an understanding that entrepreneurial behavior is an essential element in the development of the small business sector; thirdly, an ability to identify traits common to successful entrepreneurs; and fourthly, they will develop and practice a vari-

Alina M. Zapalska is Professor of Economics, Division of Finance and Economics, Marshall University, 400 Hall Greer Boulevard, Huntington, WV 25755-2320 (E-mail: zapalska@marshall.edu) and Geoff Perry is affiliated with AGL-Economics, Business Faculty, Auckland University of Technology, Private Bag 92006, Auckland 1020, New Zealand (E-mail: Geoff.Perry@aut.ac.nz).

[Haworth co-indexing entry note]: "Collaborative Learning Instrument in Teaching Entrepreneurship Issues." Zapalska, Alina M., and Geoff Perry. Co-published simultaneously in *Journal of Teaching in International Business* (International Business Press, an imprint of The Haworth Press, Inc.) Vol. 13, No. 3/4, 2002, pp. 57-76; and: *International Business Teaching in Eastern and Central European Countries* (ed: George Tesar) International Business Press, an imprint of The Haworth Press, Inc., 2002, pp. 57-76. Single or multiple copies of this article are available for a fee from The Haworth Document Delivery Service [1-800-HAWORTH 9:00 a.m. - 5:00 p.m. (EST). E-mail address: getinfo@haworthpressinc.com].

ety of entrepreneurial skills themselves that may make them aware of their potential as entrepreneurs. *[Article copies available for a fee from The Haworth Document Delivery Service: 1-800-HAWORTH. E-mail address: <getinfo@haworthpressinc.com> Website: <http://www.HaworthPress.com>*

KEYWORDS. Collaborative learning, entrepreneurship, Central and Eastern Europe

INTRODUCTION

Since the events in the 1989 when the communist regimes of Eastern Europe collapsed, economic reforms in the countries of Central and Eastern Europe (CEE) have created new challenges and opportunities for the business community. After decades of economic isolation countries of the CEE region are still developing the institutions necessary for capitalist development, the "economic way of thinking" which typifies western economies and are still striving to integrate themselves into the world's markets. One of the most important prerequisites for successful transformation is the existence of a thriving private sector and the associated entrepreneurial skills and attributes. A major contribution to this transformation can be made by the education sector and in particular by the teaching of business and entrepreneurship in a manner that will facilitate effective learning.

However, in the CEE, forms of tertiary teaching remain essentially the same as before the economic transformations took place (Rust 1994, Mitter 1992, Evans 1995) whereby teaching is typically a passive experience with memorization of concepts and facts an important component. The lack of textbooks and resource materials (Berend 1980, Koucky 1996, Nikandrov 1991, Kuebart 1989, Lindahl 1998, Sadlak 1990, Szekely 1986, Read 1995, Mitchell 1977, Madhavan 1992) and often the lack of lecturer familiarity with alternative approaches have contributed to a largely lecture-based approach. As a result many business students find the material irrelevant, difficult, and abstract (Apanasewicz 1976, Beresford-Hill 1998) and consequently, the approach is not effective.

The implications of ineffective learning by business students in economies that are trying to create vibrant private sectors are large. In order to ensure students learn effectively, the authors strongly support the integration of theory with current events, and further, that the best way to motivate students to learn a subject is to demonstrate how it is used in practice (Cheryl 1999, Cerch 1995, Hilosky 1999, Levin 1998, Nikiforuk 1996, Oskarasson 1996, Rust 1994)). To this end the authors have developed a collaborative learning instrument that allows students to assess the importance of the private sector and the role of entrepreneurship in a free market economy, and to recognize their roles in the process of systemic transformation that needs to take place in the post-communist economies.

The paper, therefore, provides details of a collaborative learning instrument that can be used in business education in CEE countries. The first section discusses the nature and importance of entrepreneurship education in business courses. In the second the theoretical justification for using a collaborative instrument is identified and following this the instrument and methods of implementation are outlined in section four. The final section includes an evaluation of the usefulness of the collaborative learning instrument.

THE ESSENTIAL ELEMENTS FOR ENTREPRENEURSHIP IN BUSINESS AND ECONOMICS EDUCATION

Entrepreneurship as a field in college education is relatively young discipline. While the field has attained the greatest rate of growth in the United States, international interest in entrepreneurship education has grown with the recognition of practical approach (Michaelson 1998, Crawford 1997, Rushing et al. 1998). Business schools in Australia and other Asian countries have recently launched new programs in entrepreneurship as well as new journals specifically addressing entrepreneurship issues (Service 1997). There are a number of key elements in entrepreneurship education with two of the main ones described below.

The first key element in entrepreneurship education is that all students understand why entrepreneurs are important to the economy of any country. Entrepreneurs create job opportunities, initiate the production process, and are catalysts who generate wealth and a higher standard of living. Without entrepreneurs resources remain unused or underutilized. The entrepreneur perceives unmet needs in the marketplace for goods and services or for new technologies, as well as innovating through technological or managerial change (Schumpeter 1979, Weber 1949).

The second key element of entrepreneurial education is to prepare students for career success, and to increase their capacity for future learning. Equally important are the learner's personal fulfillment and contribution to society. The ultimate measure of entrepreneurship education is how well it fosters all these aspirations. Virtually every career in business involves some combination of knowledge, and people skills, but few involve the integration and combination of all functional knowledge and skills to the extent that entrepreneurial activity does.

Education curriculum in the area of entrepreneurship, therefore, includes these key elements. A typical small business course in entrepreneurship includes coverage of most or all of the following major areas: the small business environment; initiating a small business; basic management considerations; marketing considerations; financial and administrative considerations; legal an government considerations; operating typical kinds of small businesses; sources of small business assistance; characteristics of successful small business entrepreneurs and managers among many others (Kent 1996, Parker 1996). Students studying these courses should acquire knowledge and understand concepts related to entrepreneurship; acquire skills they can use in business situations and in the synthesis of a business plan; and identify and stimulate entrepreneurial drive, talent, and skills to become a successful entrepreneur.

RATIONALE FOR USING A COLLABORATIVE INSTRUMENT

Business educators can be most effective in teaching free enterprise by moving away from purely theoretical approaches by incorporating practical examples and situations. The use of current events of a business, political, and economic nature serve as one of the most effective teaching methods that can be employed in teaching free enterprise in the countries of CEE (Parker 1996, Kent 1996). Discussions of what is going on in the world around them can make free enterprise concepts come alive for students. People easily relate to those events and situations that have an impact upon them. The more frequently a teacher can relate free enterprise concepts to reality, the more frequently students will be able to see the necessity of becoming more literate in free enterprise. However, realism is often difficult to achieve in a classroom setting.

Nevertheless, dynamic and effective business teachers search for the right mix of teaching strategies to provide a variety of different ways for their students to learn. Among the most frequently used teaching procedures are reading assignments, class lectures, debates, discussions, application exercises, role playing, field trips, guest speakers, case problems, current events notebooks, class projects, the use of audiovisual aids, and experiential learning. Field trips, guest speakers, films, and filmstrips are only a few of the methods that can be employed to help teachers at all levels bring more realism into the study of free enterprise. Students can gain much in their appreciation of free enterprise by touring various businesses or having business leaders visit them.

Collaborative learning in the college classroom is another approach that has been strongly advocated and used to promote educational goals in teaching entrepreneurial issues (Bouton et al., 1983, Cooper et al., 1991 and 1996, Goodsell 1992, Maier et al., 1994.) By definition, collaborative learning requires students to work together in small groups to analyze, criticize, solve study problems and actively participate in the classroom instead of simply taking notes. Research strongly suggests that two essential elements of effective retention are active student involvement in learning process and social integration with other members (Astin 1993, Tinto 1993, Villa et al. 1994, Spence 1998, Silberman 1996, Kember 2000).

Collaborative learning implements each of these retention/promoting principles by allowing students to become actively engaged in the learning process and to interact with their peers. The opportunity to work regularly in groups serves to promote social integration, networking and bonding among students (Brufee 1993 and 1995). The goal of collaborative learning is to enhance students' learning and to develop students' social skills like decision-making, conflict management, and communication, which are considered the most important skills that business majors could acquire in college (Brufee 1995, Cooper 1996, Zapalska 1999a).

For a lesson to be collaborative, five basic elements must be included: positive interdependence, face-to-face promotive interaction, individual accountability, social skills, and group processing (Johnson 1990, 1991). To implement positive interdependence of the students' roles, goals, resources and rewards, students must believe that they are linked with each other in a way that one cannot succeed unless the other members of the group succeed and vice versa. Positive role interdependence is structured by assigning each student a role. For example, the reader reads the problems aloud to the group, the checker makes sure that all members can explain how to solve each problem correctly.

Face-to-face promotive interaction is the second basic element of a collaborative lesson. This exists among students when they help, assist, encourage, and support each other's effort to learn. They promote each other's learning by orally explaining to each other the nature of the concepts and strategies being learned, by teaching their knowledge and understanding to each other.

The third basic element of collaborative learning, individual accountability, exists when each student's performance is assessed and the results are given back to the group and the individual. Common ways of structuring individual accountability include giving a test to teach students and randomly selecting one student's work to represent the effort of the entire group.

Social skills are the fourth basic element. Groups cannot function effectively without the requisite social skills that make collaborative work effective. These include skills in leadership, making decisions, building trust, communicating, and managing conflict.

Finally, the instructor must ensure that groups "process" how well they are achieving their goals and maintaining effective working relationships among members. Successful collaborative group processing includes allowing sufficient time for the collaborative group work to occur, making the assignments specific, maintaining students' involvement in processing, reminding students to use their social skills in processing, and ensuring that expectations of the purpose of processing have been clearly communicated. According to Johnson, these five elements are what differentiate well-structured collaborative learning group from a poorly structured one (Johnson 1990, 1991).

Considerable research demonstrates that collaborative learning produces higher achievement, more positive relationships among students, and healthier psychological adjustment than do competitive or individualistic experiences (Brufee 1993). These effects, however, do not automatically appear when students are placed in groups. To be collaborative, learning groups must be carefully structured (Nevin 1994, Villa 1994).

It has been recognized that collaborative learning enables teachers to improve communications with their students, improves the students' learning, promotes higher achievement, increases critical thinking, meets the needs of students with disabilities while benefiting the other students in the classroom, enables more positive student relationships, increases individual motivation and promotes a healthier psychological environment than any other classroom method (Johnson et al., 1990 and

1991, Maier et al., 1994, Becker et al., 1995, Zapalska 1998a, 1998b, et al. 1999b.)

The research on the effects of collaborative learning suggests improvement on interpersonal measures, positive effects on academic achievement measures (improved performance on vocabulary tests, higher achievement scores on tests), and improved attitudes toward education (Sharan 1980 and et al. 1984).

It is clear that collaborative learning can accomplish a number of positive educational purposes. Our intent here is to consider some of practical aspects of using collaborative learning instrument in teaching some entrepreneurial issues.

A COLLABORATIVE INSTRUMENT APPROACH TO TEACHING ENTREPRENEURSHIP

The instrument presented is intended for use for three weeks of coursework in a one-semester course for a maximum of thirty students who have principles of economics as their only background. In order to break the monotony of lectures and dramatically change classroom dynamics, the course material is divided into small collaborative learning units.

The instructor lectures on a particular topic by providing an explicitly-stated theoretical introduction to the unit. Academic and social objectives, study procedures and a list of potential study questions are distributed to students to enable them to concentrate on important material and to better master that material. After the instructor delivers the lecture segment, collaborative learning takes place. Temporary groups are formed that last for only a unit period (50 minutes each). Students work together to analyze, discuss and solve assignment problems. The instructor works with students by monitoring their performance, helping and providing feedback when it is needed.

The authors primarily use in-class group work as this tends to be more productive than out-of class group work. To obtain a better collaborative learning environment, students are arranged in circles or clusters. The explicit collaborative learning structure is linked to a group work assignment which is part of the course assessment. This ensures promptness and productivity on the part of students via a series of activities tied to the assigned readings, traditional lectures and home assignments.

This instrument demonstrates how students can benefit from opportunities that complement lectures with active students' participation. Breaking up lectures with collaborative learning processes enhances what is learned and builds relationships and social attitudes among students in class. The project is designed to help students better understand abstract theory by relating it to real-world economic issues and problems and to help the instructor adopt a format for collaborative learning procedures that are appropriate for the classroom.

The role of an instructor in identifying and stimulating entrepreneurial drive, talent, and skill is to give students an opportunity to assess their strengths and see how well they fit with accepted characteristics of successful entrepreneurs. Although many people think entrepreneurs are born, not made, studies of company founders suggest that a variety of experiences helped these self-motivated people succeed (Zapalska 1997, Cunningham et al. 1991, Chell et al. 1991). Helping students see the importance of self-confidence and goal setting in achieving success is essential. People who start companies seem to believe that they can control their own destinies, and though their activities seem an enormous risk to uninvolved observers, the entrepreneur believes the risks are actually moderate and can be minimized (Chell et al. 1991).

At the beginning of our instrument, students view a video film on "The Entrepreneur" produced by the Educational Video Network, Inc. Huntsville, Texas. Providing a background on the role of entrepreneurship in an enterprise economy is a critical starting point for students from Central and Eastern Europe. This film is not of great value by itself if it is shown without comment or discussion. Therefore, before showing a film to a class, the instructor must see it by himself/herself to note what points it illustrates and provides some focus for students. This may be done through a handout, a verbal introduction by the instructor, a set of questions for students to make notes on or an overall question that will encourage students to view the film critically. The film becomes more valuable if students know what to look for and how to relate it to the subject matter. The film presented offers visual demonstration and illustration of entrepreneurship. Students also have an opportunity to view the film outside the class since repeating the film adds to its educational value.

By viewing the film, students learn that individual psychological profiles and actions make entrepreneurs. Personality-based theories of entrepreneurship identify those traits common to successful entrepreneurs. The list of traits is long but includes characteristics like an internal locus of control, the ability to bear the risk, the desire for responsibility, sources of formal authority and power, aggressiveness, the need for recognition, individual creativity, energy and ambition, possessing a high need for achievement and autonomy, independence, and initiative. The film demonstrates that those entrepreneurs who are innovative, hardworking, and dependable have a better chance of success than those who are not in their business activities. Whether students plan to own their own business or choose to become involved in more traditional careers, these attitudes are important in achieving success, yet they are most often overlooked in the traditional business curriculum (Zapalska et al. 1999b).

Based on the information from viewing the video on "American Entrepreneur," each student is given a homework assignment. They are asked to list all viewed entrepreneurs and provide twenty personality traits and distinctive characteristics relevant to their success. During the next class, students work collaboratively on in-class assignment where they again are asked to complete a description of all entrepreneurs, write personal views regarding entrepreneurs' characteristics and attributes, evaluate their practices, and provide their own definition of an American entrepreneur. Specifically, students are asked to define an entrepreneur and state the role he/she plays in free market economy and to select a list of ten attributes and characteristics that are the most common for a successful American entrepreneur. Students have approximately forty-five minutes to complete their group task. Reports on assigned work are due at the end of class.

The unit can be finalized with a visiting entrepreneur who provides a welcome change of pace in the course routine. For maximum success, students are prepared for the visitor and some efforts are made to get the class to formulate the questions that the entrepreneur will attempt to answer. The visitor is asked to allow some of the class period for questions so students can follow up the questions formulated before the visit. Ad hoc questions are also expected. Part of the following class period is allotted to discussion of the visitor's contribution.

The second part of the collaborative instrument's academic objective is to provide information necessary to appraise the rising entrepreneurial class in the economies of CEE. The main point is to allow students to contrast American capitalist entrepreneurship with entrepreneurship in Poland. At the beginning of class, the instructor stresses that Poland is regarded as a front-runner in the recent wave of economic reforms sweeping CEE. The economic transformation program was launched with the now legendary big bang on January 1, 1990 which substantially freed prices and lowered entry barriers. The response of the economy was huge with the share of the private sector in economic activity growing rapidly. The decisive liberalization accompanying the big bang was instrumental in pointing out the shape of new opportunities. Despite many positive effects that systemic transformation brought about in the CEE counties, the new class of Polish entrepreneurs faces the usual problems one would expect for an economy in transition.

The lecturer provides materials on Polish entrepreneurs for the students to analyze. These materials are drawn from Wyznikiewicz (et al. 1993) who present a quick overview of private sector development, a summary of the main patterns emerging from the surveyed entrepreneurs and detailed profiles of fifty Polish entrepreneurs. An example of one of the stories on Polish entrepreneurs is presented in Table 1. Based on these materials, students collaboratively work in groups to list all the entrepreneurs covered and to provide for each entrepreneur a list of ten distinctive characteristics relevant to their success. They are also asked to provide a definition for an entrepreneur in Poland, and state the roles they play in the transforming Polish economy. A group report on the above assignment is supposed to be turned in at the end of class. There are approximately forty-five minutes to complete this assignment. Students' work in collaboration on one of the assignments is presented in Table 2.

When forming the groups, the authors did not allow students to form their own groups or deliberately create homogeneous groups. The authors did not want to establish groups that were either too small (three or fewer members) or too large (six or more members). The authors noticed that groups of less than three can be too small for a stimulating interaction, especially when some members are absent. Larger groups limit the amount of time individuals can speak. An upper limit of three members is imposed to encourage face-to-face interaction, eliminate insufficient diversity of views and off-task behavior, and maintain meaningful participation of all participants. As the group with greater diversity sets the conditions for greater opportunity and new views, we form heterogeneous groups based on prior achievement, ability level, major or minor, ethnicity, and gender. Small group collaborative work is good method for allowing students to focus their thinking on an issue and problems related to entrepreneurship, explore all aspects of it, and arrive at some solution and conclusion that the students expected.

The authors dissolve and reform the groups on a frequent basis, such as after each activity or simulation. A variation on the small group is the rotating group. This method provides opportunity for students to be exposed to the thinking of more than one group of their peers. Particularly

TABLE 1. A Sample of Students' Readings on Polish Entrepreneurship

---

Andrzej Kubasiewicz, aged 57, holds a Ph.D. in engineering science, and is fluent in English, French and Russian. He is the founder and president of International Glass Plant (IGP), a successful limited liability company active in manufacturing and trading construction glass. For most of his professional career, Mr. Kubasiewicz worked for Budimex, a huge state-owned foreign trade company. Prior to the Economic Transformation Program (ETP), Budimex had a monopoly on trading building materials. Mr. Kubasiewicz left Budimex as a vice-president in 1990. In August 1990, IGP was formed as a limited liability company. The enterprise was family-owned by Kubasiewicz's brother, his son, his daughter and himself. His daughter looks after the advertising section. The bulk of the founding capital came from the brother, who lives abroad. Recently, IGP went into partnership with Pilkington, a British glass company with annual sales surpassing US $5 billion. The Kubasiewicz family owns 55 percent of the shares and Pilkington 45 percent in the joint venture. IGP employs 135 people and engages in the wholesale trade of glass, mainly construction glass, both imported and produced in its five factories in Poland. It specializes in high-quality glass that was barely available earlier and virtually unknown in the traditional Polish construction industry. It appeared together with the inflow of western capital and technologies when the ETP began. Western construction companies have been involved in Poland since the early 1970s, but their presence now is much greater than before. Poland needs modern offices and apartment buildings, hotels, exhibition halls, etc. IGP is an example of a Polish company that is joining the fray, competing with foreign companies. The glass sold by IGP satisfies West European requirements, thanks to imported technology, and received the Rosenheim certificate for the highest quality standards. Sixty percent of IGP's sales come from exports and forty percent from domestic demand. The share of the latter is growing and is likely to exceed that of imports in the near future. IGP factories also produce tools for the glass industry, for purchase by small glass workshops. According to Mr. Kubasiewicz, domestic competition (with the exception of small workshops) has been practically eliminated from important markets in Poland by IGP. New office buildings and hotels in Warsaw and other big cities built by both Polish and foreign companies use IGP glass, which is locally available and competitive with imports. All major new car salons in Warsaw and other downtown shops are equipped with glass by IGP. Kubasiewicz prefers to do business with private companies rather than with state enterprises. He cannot, however, avoid the latter, which act as suppliers to IGP. Kubasiewicz asserts that managers of state enterprises retain the mentality and behavior prevalent during the central planning era, and they do not treat private companies as serious business partners. The same attitude is encountered, according to Kubasiewicz, in many state banks in Poland. Mr. Kubasiewicz is pleased that his contacts with the state bureaucracy are limited.

TABLE 2. Study Sheet: Polish Entrepreneurship

Based on the previous assignment on Polish Entrepreneurship: (1) discuss and prepare a group report on the following questions due in the next class; (2) prepare an oral presentation of your answers to the questions. Be sure that your answers are complete and that each group member presents.

1. What is a major motive for business start-up in the economies of Central and Eastern Europe (CEE)?
2. How does business proprietorship in post-communist economies offer an attractive solution in the changing economic conditions in the 1990s?
3. What are the conditions of the economies of CEE for a start-up of small businesses in the 1990s?
4. Are these small business start-ups in CEE the trigger that is likely to lead to fundamental transformation in either the ideological or the material structures of these economies?
5. Who are those who most likely will engage in small business proprietorship or entrepreneurship?
6. What difficulties do the first entrepreneurs in the CEE face?
7. What is the role of the formation of small-scale economic enterprises in these newly-emerging market conditions of the 1990s?
8. How do these small-scale business proprietorships acquire the necessary skills of financial management?
9. What is the nature of employer-employee relations and how are various forms of employer control legitimated within such enterprise?
10. How are mechanisms of employee commitment established and how are various forms of employer legitimacy enforced?
11. How far are business proprietors committed to long-term business growth?
12. To what extent is small business ownership geared to a nation of proprietorship rather than to entrepreneurship with long-term capital accumulation of the kind discussed by Max Weber (Weber, 1949)?

---

for brainstorming on a series of questions, the method can force them to assemble their ideas quickly and efficiently. Initially, students are assigned to groups of four to five to work and discuss the questions and issues provided. For a given time period, they discuss one segment of the material. At the end of this period, selected members of the group rotate to the next group. Each group appoints the members to rotate.

In debriefing sessions, a recorder reports the ideas from each group. The advantage of this method is that the composition of different groups stimulate more ideas than if a single configuration worked on all the assignment as a group. Like most group work, this technique requires structure. The group must be able to organize quickly, decide which members will rotate, will be a leader and a recorder, and how they will proceed to tackle the assignments.

Students are required to prepare and conduct a group presentation. The task is to prepare and present an informative and interesting presentation. The collaborative goal is for all members to learn the material being presented and to gain experience in making presentations. The individual accountability is for all members to participate equally in the presentation. To ensure that each student is individually accountable to do his or her fair share of the group's work, the authors had to assess how much effort each member was contributing to the group's work, provided feedback to groups and individual students, helped groups to avoid redundant efforts by members, and ensured that every member is responsible for the final outcome. To further ensure individual accountability, the authors gave an examination and selected group members at random to explain how to solve randomly selected issue from the collaborative group assignment.

Occasional reporting by the students to the whole class (by randomly calling on individual students to report for their group) helped the authors guide the overall flow of the class. Carefully monitoring the collaborative groups and using formal observation sheet to collect concrete data on the groups' functioning facilitated whole-class and small-group processing.

When formulating grading policies, the authors left out any form of peer evaluation in the grading system, but maximized the extent to which group performance affected students' grades. Students understood course requirements and were committed to a grading system that provided incentives for group work, and also stimulated within each of the groups a discussion about individual constraints and the degree to which they might affect their ability to perform effectively.

Students write their reports in individual groups. When the papers are completed, members of the group proofread each other's composition, correcting capitalization, punctuation, spelling, use of language, use of topic, sentence, organization, and conceptualization, and suggesting how to improve other aspects of the paper. The criterion for success is a well-written composition by each group. The report is evaluated for grammar, punctuation organization, and content. When the papers are completed, members of the collaborative group discussed how effectively they had worked together by listing the specific actions they had engaged in to help each other.

EVALUATION OF THE APPROACH

During the spring semester of 2001, the authors distributed this 10-item survey to the 25 students enrolled in an undergraduate Economics Principles class at Marshall University, Huntington, West Virginia. An instrument that we used to validate entrepreneurship education effectiveness is presented in Table 3. This uniform method of evaluation enables the lecturer to measure students' satisfaction and impact on students' attitudes towards entrepreneurship. In addition, the survey contained one-open ended item where the students were asked to provide any comments related to the course and the collaborative technique used in this course.

Table 3 presents the evaluation results by reporting a frequency count of the specific impact on the students' attitudes towards entrepreneurship before and after they participated in the collaborative activity. Students were asked to report their least positive and most positive experience on a scale from 1 to 5 respectively.

According to the results, the effectiveness of the collaborative technique on teaching entrepreneurial issues has been documented by both positive teaching evaluations and student feedback. The course effect on students' appreciation and attitude towards entrepreneurship was rated highly. As the results indicate that students' desires to start or buy a business, students' confidence in their ability to start or run and buy a business have improved substantially after the students completed the exercise. They also expressed a greater appreciation of their own skills to become successful entrepreneurs, and greater needs to learn more in order to become a successful entrepreneur. When asked about their potential for becoming successful entrepreneurs and for finding and identifying business opportunities most of the students expressed greater confidence in both.

From students' comments, we also learned that they enjoyed learning facts about entrepreneurship and the role of small entrepreneurial firms in the economies of different level of entrepreneurial development. Students also benefited from collaborative learning in a few important ways. They all expressed a great appreciation for having the non-theoretical nature of the class. Students indicated that they learned more and retain their knowledge longer because of their active involvement in the learning process and the constant feedback to students from both instructor and other students. They also expressed that they liked having the course divided into small units with rotation of group members that provided more efficient learning and performance. The collaborative

TABLE 3. Sample of Questions and Answers to Assess Effectiveness of Entrepreneurial Education

Please rate yourself on each of the following items based on a 5-point scale ranging from 1 = none to 5 = a great amount.

	1 = none	2	3	4	5 = great amount
	(Responses in percentages)				
1. Desire to start a business someday:					
Before the class	48	26	24	2	-
After the class	15	34	46	5	-
2. Desire to buy a business someday or to start an entrepreneurial career:					
Before the class	38	31	23	8	-
After the class	15	25	47	10	3
3. Confidence in your ability to start and run a business:					
Before the class	44	37	17	2	-
After the class	20	54	19	7	-
4. Confidence in your ability to buy and run the business:					
Before the class	22	26	25	27	-
After the class	5	39	43	13	-
5. Your skill level to become a successful entrepreneur:					
Before the class	28	35	37	-	-
After the class	10	49	31	9	1
6. How much more do you think you need to learn to become a successful entrepreneur?					
Before the class	-	1	11	54	34
After the class	-	-	-	67	33
7. Evaluate yourself as a potential successful entrepreneur:					
Before the class	34	24	32	10	-
After the class	20	31	20	28	1
8. Your ability to identify and evaluate business opportunities:					
Before the class	15	35	39	11	-
After the class	-	30	42	25	3
10. Your level of satisfaction with this course unit	-	-	6	68	26
Comments about the course:					

instrument on the entrepreneurial issues provided the students with tools they can use in any career whether or not they elect to open their own business.

They all were actively involved in the learning process, received immediate feedback, and had an opportunity to work on challenging and completely new problems with their peers. By having opportunities to work collaboratively, use knowledge, make decisions, discuss problems, conduct research to discover and create new knowledge, a number of critical thinking processes emerged.

Collaborative teamwork also fostered friendship and social support and gave students an opportunity to develop interpersonal and group skills. It also increased motivation, interest level and excitement, and gave students a chance to take control of their own learning and gain confidence and effectiveness in finding more and better solutions to problems. It also prompted students to think critically, to undertake active, effective and systematic information gathering, and to organize, analyze, summarize, evaluate and draw out implications from this information.

The instrument minimized memorization and repetition and gave students opportunities to interact with other students and the instructor, question and try out different approaches and explain their own ideas while learning. Through collaborative group explorations students were pushed to analyze what they think and learn, and to discuss and clarify their own reasoning.

The authors find that business courses are very suitable for collaborative learning. Students who are exposed to small group collaborative learning find it an effective teaching method even when conducted by an instructor who has little experience and who appears better adapted to lecturing. The effectiveness of small group instruction together with the professor's lecture technique may influence its effect on course satisfaction. It is recommended that more professors in the countries of CEE experiment with small group work to ascertain their effectiveness with the collaborative teaching process. Improvement is expected to continue as collaborative learning is a dynamic and effective activity in entrepreneurial education.

CONCLUSIONS

This study illustrates the use of a collaborative learning instrument to teach entrepreneurial issues. The use of small group learning with strong collaborative interaction significantly contributes to an effective process of learning. To be collaborative, a group must have clear positive interdependence and members must promote each other's learning and success face to face, hold each other individually accountable to do his or her fair share of work, appropriately use the interpersonal and small group skills needed for cooperative efforts to be successful, and process as a group how effectively members are working together.

These five essential components were present for the small-group collaborative earning to be truly collaborative.

Entrepreneurial firms are an important component of the market economy, and interest in them should continue to grow in the CEE economies. The economic and entrepreneurial education approach facilitates an objective look at economic problems, encouraging individuals to be better decision makers not only as consumers, wage earners, citizens, and investors but also as small business owners and entrepreneurs. Entrepreneurial and economic concepts along with the development of an economic and entrepreneurial way of thinking can and should be a pervasive part of basic business education if such courses are truly meeting the objectives of business and entrepreneurial education of the 21 century.

The objectives for business education in the CEE economies include national recognition for innovative, creative, academically rigorous programs and research in entrepreneurship; greater credibility and visibility of the school within the external business community; development of funding sources to support entrepreneurship education. By meeting the challenge and accepting the responsibility of entrepreneurial education, the revitalization of basic business programs for students in the CEE will be successful. By increasing the availability of free enterprise education to potential and practicing owners and managers of entrepreneurial ventures, business educators can strengthen emerging free enterprise system and meet the great American dream that anyone who was born in the communist or post-communist economy can own and manage an entrepreneurial business in the new emerging free enterprise economy of the CEE.

REFERENCES

Apanasewicz, N. (1976). The Educational System of Poland. Education Around the World. *Social Studies* (January), 1, 19.

Astin, V. (1993) *What Matters in College?* San Francisco: Jossey-Bass.

Becker, E. W. and Watts M. (1995). Teaching Tools: Teaching Methods in Undergraduate Economics. *Economic Inquiry*, 23, 692-700.

Berend, I. (1980). Educational Reforms in East-Central Europe: the Hungarian Example, Prospects. *Quarterly Review of Education*, 10 (2), 169-173.

Beresford-Hill, P. (1998). Education and Privatization in Eastern Europe and the Baltic Republics. *Oxford Studies in Comparative Education* (January), 7 (2) 122.

Bouton, C. and Garth R. (1983). *Learning in Groups.* San Francisco: Jossey-Bass.

Brufee, K.A. (1993). *Collaborative Learning.* John Hopkins Press.

Brufee, K.A. (1995). Sharing Our Toys: Cooperative Learning Versus Collaborative Learning. *Change*, 27 (1), 12-18.

Cerch, L. (1995). Educational Reforms in Central and Eastern Europe. *European Journal of Education* (December), 30 (4), 423-435.

Chell, E. (ed). (1991). *The Entrepreneurial Personality: Concepts, Cases and Categories*. London: Routledge.

Cheryl L. (1999). Cooperative Learning in a Macroeconomics Course: A Team Simulation. *College Teaching*, (Spring), 47 (2), 51-54.

Cooper, J. (1996). Research on Cooperative Learning in the Mid 1990s: What the Experts Say? *Cooperative Learning and College Teaching*, 6 (2), 2-3.

Cooper, J., McKinney, M. and Robinson, P. (1991). Cooperative, Collaborative Learning: Part II. *Journal of Staff Program and Organization Development*, 9 (4), 241-252.

Crawford, G. (ed.). (1997). A Business View of Economics Education: the Need to Balance Application and Theory in the Classroom (Fall), 13 (1), 126-139.

Cunningham, J. B. (ed). (1991). Defining Entrepreneurship. *Journal of Small Business Management*, 29 (1) 45-61.

Evans, F. (ed). (1995). Business Education and Change in Russia and Eastern Europe. *Journal of Education For Business* (January/ February), 70 (3), 166-172.

Goodsell, A. (ed.) (1992). *Collaborative Learning: A Source-book for Higher Education*. University Park, PA: National Center For Post-secondary Teaching, Learning, and Assessment.

Hilosky, A. (ed.) (1999). *Service Learning: Brochure Writing for Basic Level College Students*. College Teaching (Fall), 47 (4) 143-147.

Johnson, D.W. and Johnson, R. (1990). *Cooperation and Competition: Theory and Research*. Edina, Minnesota: Interaction Book Company.

Johnson, D.W. and Johnson, R. (1991). *Creative Learning Cooperation in the College Classroom*. Edina, Minnesota: Interaction Book Company.

Kember, D. (2000). Action Learning and Action Research: Improving the Quality of Teaching and Learning, London: Kogan Page.

Kent C.A. (1996). Innovations in Instruction for Business and Related Subjects: The Unfinished Agenda. *Journal of Private Enterprise* (March-April), 12 (2) 1-11.

Koucky, J. (1996). Educational Reforms in Changing Societies: Central Europe in the Period of Transition. *European Journal of Education*, (March), 31 (1), 7-24.

Kuebart, F. (1989), Soviet Education and Comparative Research. *Comparative Education*, 25 (3), 283-292.

Levin, B. (1998). International Educational Reform: From Proposal to Results. *Alberta Journal of Educational Research* (Spring), 44, 1, 91-93.

Lindahl, R.A. (1998). Reflections on Educational Reform in Cuba. *International Journal of Educational Reform* (October), 7 (4), 300-308.

Madhavan, R. (ed). (1992). In Support of Reform: Western Business Education in Central and Eastern Europe. *Review of Business* (Spring), 13 (4), 4-6.

Maier, M. H. and Keenan, D. (1994). Cooperative Learning in Economics. *Economic Inquiry* (April), 358-361.

Michaelsen L. K. (1998). The Integrated Business Core: An Experiential Approach for Private Enterprise (Fall), 14 (1) 106-114

Mitchell, G. E. (1977). Glimpses of Education in Poland and Romania. *American Education* (April), 13 (3) 16-24.

Mitter, W. (1992). *Education in Eastern Europe and the Former Soviet Union in a Period of Revolutionary Change: An Approach to Comparative Analysis.* Oxford Studies in Comparative Education, 2 (1) 15-28.

Nevin, A.I. (ed.) (1994). *Creativity and Collaborative Learning: A Practical Guide to Empowering Students and Teachers.* Paul H. Brookes Publishing Co.

Nikandrov, N. (1991). Educational Developments in Russia Since 1991. *Staff and Educational Development International* (May), 1 (1) 29-37.

Nikiforuk, A. (1996). Better Read Than (Brain-)Dead. *Canadian Business* (March), 69 (3), 111-113.

Oskarsson, B. (ed) (1996). *Vocational Education and Training in Kyrgyzstan, Managing Educational reforms in an Economy in Transition*, report: European Training Foundation, Turin, Italy, (October).

Parker P.K. (1996). Contemporary Issues in Management. *Journal of Private Enterprise* (Spring 1996), 12 (2), 177-178.

Read G.H. (1995). Russian Education: The Rise of a Meritocracy. *Career Education* (Fall), 60 (1), 46-55.

Rushing, F. W. (ed). (1998). *Education in Transition From School to the Workplace: Challenges and Opportunities For Private Enterprise Education.* Journal of Private Enterprise Education (Fall), 14 (1), 29-44.

Rust V.D. (ed). (1994) International Perspectives on Education and Society, Educational Management. *Educational Reform in International Perspective* (January), 4, 275.

Sadlak, J. (1990). The Eastern European Challenge: Higher Education for a New Reality *Educational record* (Spring), 71 (2), 30-31, 34-37.

Schumpeter, J. (1934). *The Theory of Economic Development.* Cambridge, MA: Harvard University Press.

Service, R.W. (1997). Innovativeness in University Business School Teaching. *Journal of Private Enterprise*, 13 (1) 158-161.

Sharan, S. (1980). Cooperative Learning In Small Groups: Recent Methods and Effects on Achievement, Attitudes and Ethnic Relations. *Review of Educational Research*, (50), 241-271.

Sharan, S., Kussell, P., Hertz-Lazarowitz, R., Bejarano, Y., Raviv, S. and Sharan, Y. (1984). *Cooperative Learning in the Classroom: Research in Desegregated Schools.* Hillsdale, N.J.: Lawrence Erlbaum Associates.

Silberman, M.L. (1996). *Active Learning; 101 Strategies to Teach Any Subject.* Boston: Allyn and Bacon.

Spence, J. T. (1998). *Action Learning for Individual and Organizational Development: Practice Application Brief.* Columbus, OH: Eric Clearinghouse on Adult, Career, and Vocational Education, Center on Education and Training For Employment, College of Education, the Ohio State University.

Szekely, B.B. (1986). The New Soviet Educational Reform. *Comparative Education Review*, 30, (3), 321-343.

Tinto, V. (1993) *Learning College, Rethinking the Causes and Curves for Student Attrition.* Chicago, University of Chicago Press.

The Entrepreneurs. 1995. Educational Video Network, Inc. Huntsville, Texas.

Villa, R.A.(ed) (1994). *Creativity and Cooperative Learning: A Practical Guide to Empowering Students and Teachers.* Paul H. Brookes Publishing Co.

Weber, M. (1949). *The Methodology of the Social Sciences.* The Free Press of Glencoe, Illinois.

Wyznikiewicz, B. and Pinto, B. (1993). *Coping with Capitalism, Discussion Paper 18.* The World Bank and International Finance Corporation.

Zapalska, A (1997). Profiles of Polish Entrepreneurship. *Journal of Small Business Management* (April) 35 (2), 11-117.

Zapalska, A. and Fogel, G. (1998a). Profiles of Polish and Hungarian Entrepreneurship. *Journal of Enterprise Education* (Spring), 13(2) 124-132.

Zapalska, A. and Brozik, D. (1998b). *The Money Game, Teaching Economics: Instruction and Classroom Based Research.* McGraw Hill & Robert Morris College (February), 101-113.

Zapalska, A. and Zapalska, L. (1999a). Small Business Ventures in Post-communist Hungary. *Journal of East-West Business*, 5 (4) 5-22.

Zapalska, A. and Brozik, D. (1999b). Interactive Classroom Economics Learning: The Market Game. *Social Studies* (December), 90 (6) 278-282.

Learning Styles

Alina M. Zapalska
Helen Dabb

SUMMARY. The purpose of this paper is to describe an assessment instrument that college professors can use to identify their own teaching strategies as well as to help their students become more aware of their own learning strategies and motivation for learning. The learning styles of students in two different sections of business-economics courses at Marshall University (MU), Huntington, West Virginia, and Auckland Institute of Technology (AIT), Auckland, New Zealand are determined via the use of the VARK instrument. The information generated by the instrument informs about the general cognitive and motivational characteristics of their students. This information in turn can be used in course planning and teaching. The achievement of college students could be improved by providing instruction in a manner consistent with each student's learning style. The VARK instrument could provide both students and educators in the countries of Central and Eastern Europe with a stimulus for reflection and a change in both learning and teaching methods. *[Article copies available for a fee from The Haworth Document Delivery Service: 1-800-HAWORTH. E-mail address: <getinfo@haworthpressinc.com> Website: <http://www. HaworthPress.com> © 2002 by The Haworth Press, Inc. All rights reserved.]*

Alina M. Zapalska is Professor of Economics, Lewis College of Business, Marshall University, 400 Hal Greer Blvd., Huntington, WV 25755-2320 (E-mail: zapalska@marshall.edu) and Helen Dabb is Senior Lecturer, Faculty of Business, Auckland University of Technology, Private Bag 92006, Auckland 1020. New Zealand (E-mail: helen.dabb@aut.ac.nz).

[Haworth co-indexing entry note]: "Learning Styles." Zapalska, Alina M., and Helen Dabb. Co-published simultaneously in *Journal of Teaching in International Business* (International Business Press, an imprint of The Haworth Press, Inc.) Vol. 13, No. 3/4, 2002, pp. 77-97; and: *International Business Teaching in Eastern and Central European Countries* (ed: George Tesar) International Business Press, an imprint of The Haworth Press, Inc., 2002, pp. 77-97. Single or multiple copies of this article are available for a fee from The Haworth Document Delivery Service [1-800-HAWORTH 9:00 a.m. - 5:00 p.m. (EST). E-mail address: getinfo@haworthpressinc.com].

KEYWORDS. Teaching strategies, assessment, educators, Central and Eastern Europe

INTRODUCTION

The past decade has been seeing a revival of market forces in the economies of Central and Eastern Europe by a wave of enterprise re-structuring, new developments of business and adoption of new technology. Much of the recent work on the restructuring of the East European economies has focused on economic, political, and social issues. In this paper, we argue that market transitions of the post-socialist economies of Central and Eastern Europe (CEE) cannot be successful without similar system restructuring of an education system.

To address the massive problems that still plague the educational system in the post-reform economies of CEE, the governments of the region must promote reforms of the college educational system. The governments of the CEE countries should recommend changes at the university level curriculum and strategies of instructional methodologies.

One of the important aspects of educational reform in CEE is to educate college professors about the students *learning styles.* Understanding how students learn is an important part of selecting appropriate teaching strategies. Such knowledge can assist college professors in adjusting their teaching styles to the students' *learning styles.* College lectures should be structured so that all *learning styles* are addressed, enabling every student to become actively engaged in the lessons. When the curriculum is integrated around a theme with proper attention given to brain compatibility, teaching strategies, and curriculum development, learning is enhanced.

The purpose of this paper is to describe an assessment instrument that college professors can use to identify their own teaching strategies as well as to help their students become more aware of their own learning strategies and motivation for learning.

The learning styles of students in two different sections of business-economics courses at Marshall University (MU), Huntington, West Virginia, Auckland University of Technology (AIT), Auckland, New Zealand, and three sections of business economics at Economic University, Krakow, Poland are determined via the use of the VARK instrument. The information generated by the instrument informs about the general cognitive and motivational characteristics of their students.

This information in turn can be used in course planning and teaching. The achievement of college students could be improved by providing instruction in a manner consistent with each student's learning style.

This paper is organized in the following order. In Section II, we define *learning style* and present literature review. In Section III, we discuss types of learning styles. In section IV, we answer the following question: how to identify learning style? The VARK instrument is discussed in section V. Section VI presents an analysis of data that is followed by results, conclusions, references, and appendices.

LITERATURE REVIEW

There are several definitions of learning styles, as well as several instruments to measure them. Grasha (1990) defined *learning styles* as "the preferences students have for thinking, relating to others, and particular types of classroom environments and experiences" (p. 26). How people prefer to learn is their *learning style preference* (Dunn et al. 1989, 1981, Canfield 1988, Kolb 1984).

The most often quoted definition of *learning style* is that of Keefe (1979). He defines the learning styles in the context of characteristics cognitive, affective and physiological behaviors that serve as relatively stable indicators of how learners perceive, interact with, and respond to the learning environment. Learning has cognitive, motivational, and behavioral elements rooted in genetic structure and personality and affected by the individual's developmental and environmental characteristics.

Cognitive styles are information processing habits representing the learner's typical mode of perceiving, thinking, problem solving, and remembering (Messick 1976). The cognitive elements are internal to the learner's information processing structure and require careful training before any lasting modification. Affective elements are preferential in nature and respond both to training and matching. Physiological elements are rooted in learner reactions to the environment and are most responsive to matching strategies (Ebeling 2001, Keefe 1982, Biberman et al. 1986).

The initial research on learning styles reinforces the central theme that variations in student learning style have important implications for the instructional process (Keefe 1982, Messick 1976). In effect, some *learning styles* are better developed and more likely to be preferred. The others are somewhat dormant, in need of exercise, and may surface with sufficient support. Some learners may be more independent or less dependent, or the competitive or collaborative aspects of their styles may dominate. Differences in *learning styles* are a result of such things as past life experiences, genetic make-up, life and educational experiences, and the demands of the present environment (Manner 2001, Kolb, 1984, Dunn at el. 1993, 1990).

Preferences for learning styles change over time (Dunn et al. 1993, Fleming 1992, 1995a and 1995b). However, during a period in which an individual has strong style preferences, that person will achieve most easily when taught with strategies and resources that complement those preferences (Dunn et al. 1993, Fleming 1995a, et al. 1995b, and et al. 1992, Galloway 1984, Diaz et al. 1999). According to Gregoric the potential for both style "match" and "clash" between teacher and learner must be considered (Gregoric 1985a, 1985b).

Research on *learning styles* of college students in various disciplines has also been reported (Canfield 1988, Butler 1988). Biberman (et al. 1986) examines learning styles within the area of business and finds that the styles of majors in accounting and economics/finance vary from majors in marketing and management. A significant body of research conducted by Dunn (1981, 1989) indicates that the differences among *learning styles* become more striking as our learning communities in higher education have become more diverse.

The most recent research on learning questions how particular type of technology influences the *learning styles* of students and how to use that information in designing a course to provide a theoretical justification for the method (Manner 2001, Grasha 1994, Dille at el. 1991, Gee 1990, Farmer 1995, Ross 1999).

The implication of the work on *learning styles* and technology is that students who prefer, and benefit from, learning in technologically based courses are different from those who prefer more traditional courses. Many studies suggest that the students interested in technology-based courses are independent learners who prefer a more abstract way of thinking. Such characteristics, however, do not represent the majority of college students (Cohen 1997). Those promoting technology in courses must recognize that not every student will easily benefit from its use (Grasha 1990, 1994, 1996, Lowman 1994).

In contrast, Farmer argues that if teachers are going to use technology as a teaching tool, they must consider the instructional design process and understand *leaning styles* as they relate to their students. As teachers begin to understand *learning styles*, it becomes apparent why multimedia-based instruction appeals to learners and is an effective teaching methodology. Students learn differently from each other, so mix of media satisfies the many types of learning preferences that one person may embody or that a class embodies (Farmer 1995).

Similarly, the work by Ross et al. (1999) on the relationship of learning style to Web-based learning reports that the way course information is presented and assignments are structured on the World Wide Web can cater to different sensory, social, and thinking styles of students. The authors provide numerous illustrations of how an online course might structure information to make it compatible with the needs of various types of learners. As it would be impractical to design a course for only one *learning style*, a better option is using an electronic format with variety in how information is presented or assignments are structured.

One outgrowth of *learning style* research has been the interest in applied modes of learning style. Researchers are attempting to assess *learning styles* in an effort to improve the efficiency and effectiveness of instructional materials and methods. Many of the learning style theories have spawned assessment tools that can be used to categorize learners according to the parameters of the respective theory and match students with teachers and approaches that are suited to their learning styles (Keefe 1982, Grasha 1994).

TYPES OF LEARNING STYLES

According to several authors learning modes have different characteristics but tend to overlap in many respects (Dunn 1993). Gregoric (1985a) and Butler (1988) use a theory that identifies learning style in terms of the following modes: concrete, abstract, sequential, and random.

Concrete learners need to be involved in learning a concept in a real way, where concrete objects are used. It is critical for those learners to be physically involved with a new concept or new information. Abstract learners tend to be precise and attentive to specific details. They take pieces of information and data to synthesize them together to understand concepts as a whole.

Sequential learners are structured and ordered. The learning process must be clear and precise, specific details need to be clearly delineated, and concrete steps have to be specifically outlined.

Random learners, are holistic by nature and not ordered or structured. They cannot operate in a structural way in learning situations but prefer to be "all over the place" in their attempt to understand something new (Sims et al. 1995).

Similarly, Sousa identifies three primary learning styles that make up the learners in our classrooms (Sousa 1995, 1997, 1999). The first style is *auditory*. Auditory learners are those who remember best information that they hear. Information that is auditory is processed and stored in the temporal lobes on the sides of the brain (Jensen, 1998). These students make up about 20 percent of the classroom. They like lecture, adapt well to it, and tend to be successful in our traditional schools.

The second type of learning style is *visual*. Visual information is processed and stored in the occipital lobe at the back of the brain (Jensen 1998). Visual learners are those who need a mental model that they can see. Since majority of learners are visual learners, we need to find ways to show them visually how things work.

One of the most effective tools for visual learners are graphic models, sometimes called concrete models. They help students understand and remember concepts that are difficult to visualize otherwise. Students who have difficulty with abstract concepts can be helped by the use a set of visual models that take the abstract to the concrete (Zapalska et al. 2000). By taking the information that they know and placing it in a concrete model, students are able to transfer abstract thoughts to concrete ideas more easily. Concrete models can be used at any time during the learning process but are critical in the phase of the lesson in which the teacher wants the students to use the information in some way.

The third learning style is *kinesthetic*. Kinesthetic information is stored at the top of the brain in the motor cortex until permanently learned then it is stored in the cerebellum, the area below the occipital lobe (Jensen 1998). Kinesthetic learners learn best through movement and touching. Therefore, providing opportunities for your students to work outside the classroom, by being on field trips, to make students move around the classroom, play games and simulations, is the best way to teach kinesthetic learners (Zapalska et al. 1998, et al.1999, et al. 2000, Sousa 1997, 1999).

Fleming (1995b) has further modified these three sensory preferences, specifically the visual sense by disaggregating its components into visual information presented as text, a read/write preference (R), from pictures such as diagrams and video, a visual preference (V).

IDENTIFYING LEARNING STYLES

The first step in understanding students' learning is to do a preliminary analysis of their learning styles. Some understanding of the learning styles of students can be gained through brief and personal interviews with students and discussions about how they remember simple things in their lives. The formal observation of their specific behaviors can be used to observe students while they were completing their tasks in the classroom. The instructor records exactly how each student approaches a task. The behavior of students in a classroom can tell us a considerable amount about their learning styles.

In-depth personal interviews that we conducted in our students at both Marshall University and Auckland Institute of Technology were an excellent way to find out about our students' experiences as learners. Their narratives were a rich source of information about attitudes toward teaching and learning, learning processes, and preferences for instructional techniques. While somewhat time consuming, interviews yield a great deal of qualitative data about learning styles.

The next step in working with learning styles is to help students understand how they learn best. Students need to understand that everyone has preferences in learning, but that each person's preferences are different. It is important to explain to students that learning styles are based on complex reactions to many different things in their lives, including feelings, routines, and events. As a result, patterns often develop and repeat whenever anyone concentrates on new and difficult material.

In our classrooms, we used checklists, and the VARK questionnaire (Appendix A). When we understood how both our students and we learn best, we were able to use that knowledge in planning and implementing more effective learning experiences during classroom sessions. We continued to observe each student throughout the semester in order to have the most complete picture of how he or she learns, and then both modify our teaching strategies and develop more diversified students' strategies whenever necessary.

We also kept in mind that even if each student learns best in a certain way, he or she should be exposed to a variety of learning experiences to become a more versatile learner and to be better prepared for the "real world" and life-long learning processes. Whichever method we used to help students understand how they learn we kept it brief and simple. We did not want to detract our students from the goals and objectives of the class or group teaching session. As students identified their styles, they started to examine their learning strategies within the context of their learning experiences and the extent to which certain strategies and approaches have succeeded or failed.

METHOD AND PROCEDURE:
THE VARK QUESTIONNAIRE

To accurately identify students' learning styles teachers must have a reliable and valid instruments for identifying learning styles that would do more than identify one or two variables on a bipolar continuum. A comprehensive instrument enhances the teacher's ability to prescribe instructional alternatives and the student's for significant academic improvement (Campbell et al. 1996).

There are more than a dozen commercially-published instruments that can be used to assess the different dimensions of learning style (Dunn 1993). The instruments vary in length, format, and complexity. Some require special training to administer and interpret, whereas others can be given by following a few simple directions. Some instruments measure just one dimension of style, whereas others measure two, three or more. Though the different instruments have many similarities and attempt to measure learning style preferences, the terminology used to label the learning styles varies widely (Furhman et al. 1983).

We adopted and used the VARK questionnaire that has been developed and used by Neil Fleming at Lincoln University, Canterbury, New Zealand, in 1995. The VARK instrument provides four styles of learning, called: *V, A, R, K* throughout our paper. According to Fleming, author of the VARK instrument (1995), the most common mode for information exchange is speech that arrives at the learner's ear and therefore is coded as *aural (A)* in the questionnaire. Some students reveal preferences for accessing information from printed words. This group of learners is coded as *read/writers (R)* since *reading* and *writing* are their preferred modes for receiving information. The third group of students is coded as *visual (V)* since those students like information to arrive in the form of graphs, charts, and flow diagrams. They prefer to learn by picturing information or enhancing it via colors and layout. The last group of students likes to experience their learning by using all their senses, including touch, hearing, taste, smell, and sight. This group is coded as *kinesthetic (K)*. Learners from this group like concrete, multi-sensory experiences in their learning. Learning by doing is strongly preferable, and an abstract material must be presented to them via suitable analogies, real-life examples, or metaphors. No student or teacher is restricted to only one of the four modes: V, A, R, or K. Both students and teachers may exhibit a strong preference for one particular mode and at the same time they may have a relative weakness or strength in some other modes.

The VARK instrument is a self-reported questionnaire of 13 questions that allows students to describe the features of their educational experience that they most prefer (Appendix A). Each question has four choices that the student has to select.

Before students complete the questionnaire, they should be advised to make a selection (V, A, R or K) for each question, but if necessary they may omit a question or choose two or three options. We observed that students who are strongly Read/Write in preference would probably read the instructions. Some students may fasten onto the word meanings in the questionnaire because of their orientation towards word meanings. Others with a kinesthetic preference might ask for additional contextual or situational information before they choose their answers. We tried to avoid giving further information as it might prejudice students' choices in those questions. We also indicated the use to which the data will be put and whether it remains confidential to the individual or the group.

Posting the results (preferences) for each person in a group usually leads to the following outcomes that are presented in Table 1.

Categorizing students' learning preferences was completed as follows. The first step was to find his/her total score by summing the responses of V, A, R, and K and listing from highest to lowest score. We then looked at the difference between each of the scores. We then compared this to the cut-off points for the "mode" or type of preference the student corresponds to from the VARK resource pack that is prepared by the Education Center, Lincoln University, Canterbury, New Zealand. This ranges from strong preference cut-off points, to weak preference cut-off points.

A score for a mode that stands out from the others will indicate a strong or very strong preference. Table 2 indicates a "rule of thumb" and should not be rigidly applied.

TABLE 1. An Example of Students' Responses

	V	A	R	K
Allen	10	0	3	1
Steve	6	7	4	5
Mary	7	1	8	0
Hannah	10	3	3	5

If a student's total responses are up to 16, then the difference between responses of less than two will indicate a mild preference for that mode of learning. For example, if we look at the mild preferences column in Table 2 above then a mild preference for that type of learning is indicated by a score that exceeds any other score but corresponding to the total number of responses. This is likened to a cut-off point.

To help find the Hannah's learning preferences put her responses in order from highest to lowest. These were 10, 5, 3, 3 = Total of 21. If we apply the cut-off point for a mild preference, this will mean that we are looking for a difference of 3 or greater for her total responses of 21. Thus, when we look for the difference between scores, we find that the difference between the first two (highest) scores is 5. This is greater than the cut-off point, indicating that Hannah prefers one particular learning mode–in this instance Visual. She is uni-modal with a learning preference for visual learning.

It is not expected that any single learning preference or mode will be dominant or that people are only uni-modal. Some students will be bi-modal if only two learning styles are preferred. Students with three preferred learning styles will be tri-modal, and those with differences in scores below the "cut-off" points for all their scores will be multi-modal in their learning preferences. What will become apparent in a group is that some individuals may have preferences for particular learning modes while others may have preferences for other learning modes. Those students with preferences for two learning modes we refer to as bi-modal, while those with no clear preference we refer to as multi-modal. In the Table 1 above, and the cut-off points from Table 2, Steve is multi-modal (A, V, K and R). His scores were 7, 6, 5, 4 = Total of 22. The cut-off point for mild learning preference is 3 or greater. As there is no difference greater than 1, Steve is multi-modal.

TABLE 2. Determining Learning Preferences of Students

Total Number of Responses	Very Strong Preference Indicated by a Score That Exceeds Any Other Score by	Strong Preference Indicated by a Score That Exceeds Any Other Score by	Mild Preference Indicated by a Score That Exceeds Any Other Score by
Up to 16	4+	3	2
17-22	5+	4	3
23-30	6+	5	4
31+	7+	6	5

Allen has a single mode for learning–a visual preference (V). His scores were 10, 3, 1, 0 = Total of 14. The cut-off point for mild learning preference is 2. As the difference between his first and second scores is 7, this is greater than the cut-off point, indicating his preference for this type of learning. He is uni-modal, with a preference for visual learning. In fact, he has a very strong preference for this type of learning.

Mary has bi-modal learning preferences (V and R). Her scores were 8, 7, 1, 0 = 16. The cut-off point for mild preference is 2. Between the first and second scores the difference is 1, therefore, look at the difference between the next scores. This is 6, which is greater than the cut off at 2; therefore, Mary is bi-modal in her learning preferences, namely R followed by V. There is a higher threshold or "cut-off" points for strong and very strong learning preferences. We paid particular attention to zero scores on any mode. We noticed that zero scores are unusual and the respondent will often have an interesting story to tell.

The validity of the VARK instrument has been determined in two ways. The first is the power of the instrument to discriminate meaningful group of differences in learning style preferences. Canfield (1988) reported that administrators of this instrument give solid preliminary evidence that the preferences discriminated by scales do relate to the academic and career choices of those tested. The second evidence is whether teaching a student with techniques that match his or her learning style improves achievement and satisfaction with learning. Canfield reported a variety of studies that supported this assumption (Canfield 1988).

From our experience, the VARK instrument is recommended for adoption for several reasons. First, it alerts students and teachers to the variety of different teaching and learning approaches. Second, it focuses on one of many aspects of a full learning style–the modal preferences for learners and teachers. Third, it provides a focus for developing strategies that are tailored for individuals at the *college* level. Fourth, the VARK instrument does not attempt to define the particular strengths of individuals, but their preferences for the ways in which they like to receive and give information. Fifth, the instrument overcomes the predisposition of many educators to treat all students in a similar way.

According to the author of the VARK questionnaire, Neil Fleming, the use of this tool allows teachers to reach more students because of better match that can be reached between teacher and learner's styles. It also avoids diagnostic "labeling" but provides a basis for selecting practical strategies that both students and teachers can use (Fleming 1995a and 1995b).

ANALYSIS OF DATA

At the beginning of the first semester of 1998/99 academic year, students from the College of Business at MU and Commerce at AIT answered the VARK questionnaire. We collected questionnaires from a number of classes completing economics and business courses at various levels in New Zealand, the US, and Poland. These included Introductory Diploma level economics, Stage 3 (7000) level Applied Economics, International Economy (Stage 2 (6000)), International Trade and Finance (diploma level) at Auckland University of Technology, Auckland in New Zealand, two sections of principles of economics courses at Marshall University, Huntington, West Virginia, USA, and three sections of business economics at Academy of Economics, Krakow, Poland.[1] We calculated the percentages of the total responses that were uni-modal, bi-modal, tri-modal and multi-modal. Our sample consisted of 86 responses from NZ and 87 responses from the US,[2] a total of 173 responses. Table 3 summarizes the learning preferences for our sample, each country's sample, each class and gender for both countries combined.

According to Table 3, we found that there was a difference between the USA and NZ where multi-modal learning preferences for the USA sample were lower than for the NZ sample. There is some evidence to suggest that multi-modal preferences for learning develop through a course of study and factors such as class size and the structure of the assessment program may be a contributing factor to the development of learning preferences. We also found that the learning styles in Poland were evenly distributed among four types of learning preferences relative to the US and New Zealand. According to our results, Polish students with uni-modal learning styles were primary reading and kinesthetic learners. Our total sample (both USA and NZ) showed no gender difference in learning preferences.

It has been common knowledge that the majority of students in the CEE learn through the lecture method. According to our results, the Polish students' preferred learning style was the direct opposite of the learning from the lecture method to which they have been accustomed. Their preferred learning styles were all four types, although the majority had been previously taught by the lecture method. Those preferences indicate their desire to get directly involved in the learning experience, for example, by handling objects via games and simulations, as well as working alone toward individual goals in activities closely approximating real-world experience. They also expressed preferred conditions for

TABLE 3. Learning Styles of Students in US and New Zealand Undergraduate Business Courses

	Number of Students	Unimodal Number	Bimodal Number	Trimodal Number	Multimodal Number
Class One – USA	50	22 (44.0%)	12 (24.0%)	4 (8.0%)	12 (24.0%)
Class Two – Maori NZ	15	9 (60.0%)	0	1 (6.7%)	5 (33.3%)
Class Three – Pacific Rim NZ	16	3 (18.7%)	2 (12.5%)	0	11 (68.7%)
Class Four – International Economy NZ	27	9 (32.1%)	4 (14.3%)	1 (3.6%)	14 (50.0%)
Class Five – International Trade and Finance NZ	28	10 (37.0%)	3 (11.1%)	1 (3.7%)	13 (48.1%)
Class Six – USA	37	16 (43.2%)	5 (13.5%)	2 (5.4%)	4 (37.8%)
Class – Poland	108	32 (29.6%)	21 (19.4%)	18(16.7%)	37 (34.3%)
NZ Total	86	31 (36.0%)	9 (10.5%)	3 (3.5%)	43 (50.0%)
USA Total	87	38 (43.7%)	17 (19.5%)	6 (6.9%)	26 (29.9%)
Total Female USA and NZ	83	36 (43.4%)	12 (14.5%)	2 (2.4%)	33 (39.8%)
Total Male USA and NZ	90	33 (36.7%)	14 (15.6%)	7 (7.8%)	36 (40.0%)
Total USA, NZ and Poland	281	101(35.9%)	47(16.7%)	27(9.7%)	106(37.7%)

learning through listening to the lectures, studying on their own via reading and visual techniques.

Our findings are consistent with those of Cheng (1987). Cheng reported that most of international students in the United States must shift from the lecture method to a freer learning environment–that is, they must be exposed to solving problems instead of memorizing facts and must learn to locate information themselves instead of depending on their professors' lectures.

Since we identified four types of learners among all groups of students, particularly among Polish students, teaching strategies should represent a mix of strategies to accommodate variety of learning styles. For example, kinesthetic learners will appreciate the use games, simulations and active learning in combination with lecturing. Learners who use their visual senses would learn the best from having step-by-step instructions and directions not in an oral but written form. They also find short-term and long-term individually written assignments or combined individual assignments with some group assignments as very effective teaching instruments. Oral and written comments on homework assignments will be very effective to both aural and visual learners. Working in groups that help each other to discuss, analyze and solve problems will accommodate both aural and kinesthetic learners. Oral assignments or presentations and active participation in class discussion or group learning will help aural learners to learn fast. A use of video and computer in combination with other teaching techniques can accommodate many types of learning styles.

Today, through the use of technology, teachers are more effectively able to monitor and provide anytime, anywhere assistance to students with different learning styles. For example, through Internet students will be able to get assignments, additional help, and clarification on-line. Students who are absent or unable to attend classes can learn on-line. Students will have more learning choices as a whole world of learning opportunities becomes available.

Courses should not be limited to a single classroom space or to single building, but should be opened up to the possibilities of distance learning. Through technology, students will be able to take courses never before possible. Through technology, unlimited possibilities will make learning process more efficient for all students who posses very different learning styles.

Much software is available to the college classroom today that incorporates visual, verbal, and kinesthetic learning. Software tools allow the teacher who is unfamiliar with visual modes of learning to create them easily and effortlessly just by plugging in his or her teaching outline. Students who are visuals learners, and who need graphic presentations, will be able to view the learning in a format that is comfortable and meaningful to them.

Research projects have greater relevance when students encounter information and concepts through virtual classroom, distance learning, the Internet, and worldwide e-mail. Student projects take on a new dimension with technology as their guide. Semantic memory will be enhanced by technology because relevance or meaning will be more evident as students are able to apply information to authentic situations and problems.

Lessons can be more interesting with the addition of multimedia formats that more closely mirror the world from which our students come. Just adding Power Point presentations to low technology tools such as chalkboard and overheads would add a new dimension to teaching and learning. Moreover, technology assists with higher-level of thinking by providing a rich environment for research. The possibilities are limitless. For example, written reports can take on a new dimension when the student is able to add animation and other visuals in a Power Point or similar presentation.

An added bonus is that technology opens all the windows and doors making learning not be limited to the classroom activities. Technology that is of a high level and that mirrors the real world is the gateway to produce a quality product for students with variety of learning modes.

CONCLUSIONS

This paper supports that each student has a specific *learning style* or set of preferences and that instruction should be designed to best accommodate that unique way or combination of learning styles. The authors agree that instruction should address individual styles of learning and that some students learn best through different approaches. In order to help our students succeed, we must understand how they learn, consider how they perceive, process information, and accommodate their individual differences.

We must plan a process by which we can come to an understanding of the learning styles of our students. The plan must include thorough observations, interviews, and survey questionnaire for the students in articulating how they approach learning tasks, and experimenting with a variety of teaching strategies. The plan should be developed before students are engaged in learning experiences. When learning styles are identified, the instructor can plan appropriate teaching strategies to accommodate all individual strengths and needs.

It is very important for instructors to share information with students about their learning styles and teaching strategies to accommodate those styles. By sharing information about learning styles, we help our students gain power and control over their personal learning styles and therefore learning process.

We need to provide a number of different learning options that take into account different learning styles. Combining a mixture of approaches and teaching methods, we allow students to choose the instructions that best fit their individual learning styles. Each class should accommodate all types of learners. Effective teaching arises when teachers reach those students who are mismatched with their own learning/teaching style. The VARK instrument allows teachers to overcome this problem.

In order to teach more effectively, college professors in CEE need to know more about differences in learning styles and the complexity of the learning process of their students. They need to understand learning styles and how they relate to learning success. Instructors who know about differences in learning styles among their students are able to modify their teaching strategies and techniques to ensure that their methods, materials, and resources fit the ways in which their students learn. This in turn will maximize the learning environment and learning potential of each student.

NOTES

1. The authors would like to acknowledge the contribution of Professor Ewa Miklaszewska at Department of Finance, Economic University, Krakow, Poland, without which the data collection in Poland could not have been completed.

2. This procedure has been used in a more general study on learning preferences by the Economics Academic Group in NZ.

REFERENCES

Biberman, G., and Buchanan, J. (1986). Learning Style and Study Skills Differences Across Business and Other Academic Majors. *Journal of Education For Business* (April), 61 (7), 303-307.

Butler, K. (ed.) (1988). *Learning and Teaching Style: Theory and Practice.* Columbia CT: Learner's Dimension.

Campbell, L., Campbell, B. and Dickinson D. (1996). *Teaching and Learning Through Multiple Intelligence.* Needham Heights MA: Allyn & Bacon.

Canfield, A. (1988). *Learning Styles Inventory Manual.* Los Angeles, CA: Western Psychological Services.

Cheng, L. (1987). *Assessing Asian Language Performance: Guidelines for Evaluating Limited English Proficient Students.* Rockville, MD: Aspen.

Cohen, V.L. (1997). Learning Styles in a Technology-rich Environment. *Journal of Research on Computing in Education,* 29 (4),

Diaz, D. and Cartnar, R. (1999). Students' Learning Styles in Two Classes: Online Distance Learning and Equivalent On-campus Class. *College Teaching* (Fall), 47 (4), 130-135.

Dille, B. and Mezack M. (1991). Identifying Predictors of High Risk Among Community College Telecourse Students. *The American Journal of Distance Education* 5 (1), 24-35.

Dunn, R. (1990). Understanding the Dunn and Dunn Learning Styles Model and the Need for Individual Diagnosis and Prescription. *Reading, Writing, and Learning Disabilities,* 6, 223-247.

Dunn, R. (1993). "Teaching Gifted Adolescents Through Their Learning Style Strengths." In R. Dunn (Eds.) *Teaching and Counseling Gifted and Talented Adolescents* (pp. 37-67) Westport, CT: Praeger.

Dunn, R., Beautry, J. and Klavas A. (1989). Survey of Research on Learning Styles. *Educational Leadership* (March), 46 (6), 50-58.

Dunn, R., DeBello, T., Brennan, P. Krimsky, J., and Murrain P. (1981). Learning Style Researchers Define Differences Differently. *Educational Leadership* 38 (5), 372-375.

Ebeling, D.G. (2001). Teaching to All Learning Styles. *Education Digest* (March), 66 (7), 41-46.

Farmer, L.S. (1995). Multimedia: Multi-learning Tool. *Technology Connection* 2 (3), 30-31.

Fleming, N. (1995a) (ed). VARK–*A Resource Pack for Students and Teachers*. Lincoln University, New Zealand.

Fleming, N. (1995b). I'm Different; Not Dumb: Modes of Presentation (VARK) in the Tertiary Classroom. Paper presented at the annual conference of the Higher Education Research and Development Society of Australasia, Rockhampton, Australia.

Fleming, N and Mills C. (1992). Not another Inventory, Rather a Catalyst For Reflection. *To Improve the Academy*, 11, 137-149.

Furhman, B.S., and Grasha A.F. (1983). *A Practical Handbook For College Teachers*. Boston: Little-Brown.

Galloway, C. M. (ed). (1984). Theme Issue: Matching Teaching and Learning Styles. *Theory and Practice*, 23, (1), 58-67.

Gee. D.A. (1990). *The Impact of Students' Preferred Learning Style Variables in a Distance Education Course: Case Study. Portales*: Eastern Mexico University. (ERIC Document Reproduction Service No ED 358 836).

Grasha, A.F. (1994). A Matter of Style: The Teacher as Expert, Formal Authority, Personal Model, Facilitator, and Delegator. *College Teaching* (Fall), 42 (4), 142-149.

Grasha, A.F. (1990). Using Traditional Versus Naturalistic Approaches to Assessing Learning Styles in College Teaching. *Journal on Excellence in College Teaching*, 1, 23-38.

Grasha, A.F. (1996). *Teaching with Styles: Enhancing Learning by Understanding Teaching and Learning Styles*. Pittsburgh, PA: Alliance Publishers.

Gregoric, A.F. (1985a). *Inside Styles, Beyond the Basics*. Columbia, CT: Gregoric Associates.

Gregoric, A.F. (1985b). *Style Delineator: A Self-assessment Instrument for Adults*. Columbia, CT: Gregoric Associates.

Hativa, N. (2000). Who Prefers What? Disciplinary Differences in Students' Preferred Approaches to Teaching and Learning Styles. *Research in Higher Education* 41 (2), 209-236.

Jensen, E. (1998). *Introduction to Brain Compatible Learning*. Del Mar, CA: Turning Point.

Keefe, J. (1982). *Student Learning Styles and Brain Behavior*. Reston, VA: NASSP.

Keefe, J. (1979). "Learning Styles: An Overview." In J. Keefe (Ed.). *Student Learning Styles: Diagnosing and Prescribing Programs* (p. 1-17). Reston, VA: National Association of Secondary School Principals.

Kolb, D.A. (1984). *Experiential Learning*. Englewood Cliffs, NJ: Prentice Hall.

Lowman, J. (1994). Professors as Performers and Motivators. *CollegeTeaching* (Fall), 42 (4), 137-141.

Manner, B.M. (2001). Learning Styles and Multiple Intelligences in Students. *Journal of College Science Teaching* (March-April), 30 (6), 390-394.

Messick, S. (ed.). (1976). *Individuality In Learning*. San Francisco: Jossey-Bass.

Ross, J. and R. Schultz. (1999). Using the World-Wide Web to Accommodate Learning Style Diversity in the College Classroom. *College Teaching* (Fall), 47 (4), 123-129.

Sousa, D. (1995). *How the Brain Learns*. Reston, VA: National Association of Secondary School Principals.

Sousa, D. (1997). *How the Brain Learns: New Insights into the Teaching/Learning Process*. Reston, VA: National Association of Secondary School Principles.

Sousa, D. (1999). *How the Brain Learns*. Reston, VA: National Association of Secondary School Principals.

Sims, R.R., and Sims S.J. (1995). *The Importance of Learning Styles: Understanding the Implications For Learning Course Design and Education*. Westport CT: Greenwood Press.

Zapalska, A. and Brozik D. (1998). The Market Game. *Journal of Business and Behavioral Sciences* (Fall), 4, (1), 38-48.

Zapalska, A. and Brozik D. (1999). Interactive Classroom Economics: The Market Game. *The Social Studies* (November/December), 90 (6), 278-282.

Zapalska, A. and Brozik D. (2000). The Restaurant Game. *Simulation and Gaming* (September), 31 (3), 465-474.

APPENDIX

The VARK Questionnaire

HOW DO WE LEARN BEST?

This questionnaire aims to find out something about your preferences for the way you work with information. Choose the answer which best explains your preferences and circle the letter next to it. Please circle more than one if a single answer does not match your preferences. Leave blank any question, which does not apply.

1. You are about to give directions to a person who is standing with you. She is staying in a hotel in town and wants to visit your house later. She has a rental car. Would you:
    V)   draw a map on paper
    A)   tell her the directions
    R)   write down the directions (without a map)
    K)   collect her from the hotel in your car.

2. You are staying in a hotel and have a rental car. You would like to visit a friend whose address/location you do not know. Would you like them to:
    V)   draw you a map on paper
    A)   tell you the directions
    R)   write down the directions (without a map)
    K)   collect you from the hotel in their car.

3. You have just received a copy of your itinerary for a world trip. This is of interest to a friend. Would you:
    A)   phone her immediately and tell her about it
    R)   send her a copy of the printed itinerary
    K)   show her on a map of the world

4. You are going to cook a dessert as a special treat for your family. Do you:
    V)   thumb through the cookbook looking for ideas from the picture
    A)   ask for advice from others
    R)   refer to a particular cookbook where there is a good recipe
    K)   cook something familiar without the need for instruction

5.   A group of tourists have been assigned to you to find out about national parks. Would you:
    V)   show them slides and photographs
    A)   give them a talk on national parks
    R)   give them a book on national parks
    K)   drive them to a national park

APPENDIX (continued)

6. You are about to purchase a new stereo. Other than price, what would influence your decision?
   V)   it looks really smart and upmarket
   A)   the salesperson telling you what you want to know
   R)   reading the details about it
   K)   listening to it

7. Recall a time in your time when you learned how to do something like playing a new board game. Try to avoid choosing a very physical skill, e.g., riding a bike.
   How did you learn best? By:
   V)   visual clues–pictures, diagrams, charts
   A)   listening to somebody explaining it
   R)   written instruction
   K)   doing it or trying it

8. Which of the these games do you prefer:
   V)   pictionary
   R)   scrabble
   K)   charades

9. You are about to learn to use a new program on a computer. Would you:
   A)   telephone a friend and ask questions about it
   R)   read the manual which comes with the program
   K)   ask a friend to show you on the computer

10. You are not sure whether a word should be spelt "dependent" or "dependant." Do you:
   V)   see the word in your mind and choose by the way it looks
   A)   sound it out in your mind
   R)   look it up in the dictionary
   K)   write both versions down on paper and choose one

11. Apart from price, what would most influence your decision to buy a particular textbook:
   V)   it looks ok
   A)   a friend talking about it
   R)   skim reading parts of it
   K)   using a friend's copy

12. A new movie has arrived in town. What would most influence your decision to go (or not to go)?
   V)   you saw a preview of it
   A)   you heard a radio review about it
   R)   you read a review about it

13. Do you prefer a lecturer or teacher who likes to use:
      V)   flow diagrams, charts, slides
      A)   discussion, guest speakers
      R)   handouts and/or a textbook
      K)   field trips, labs, practical sessions

Count your choices

    Total   V __   A __   R __   K __

Companies as Business Laboratories

Miroslav Rebernik

SUMMARY. This paper shows how an effective business education program at the university level can be organized. The underlying philosophy of the program is that business education for students who will be employed by smaller companies which feature de-specialization of job tasks, resource poverty, and self-employment must be different from business education for larger companies. As part of their business education, students should gain managerial experience during their studies. Within the program described, entrepreneurs and small business owners or managers train students, and students (with the help of academicians solve real business problems. The program unites academicians and managers or entrepreneurs in pursuit of the same objective: effective small business education and training. *[Article copies available for a fee from The Haworth Document Delivery Service: 1-800-HAWORTH. E-mail address: <getinfo@haworthpressinc.com> Website: <http://www.HaworthPress.com> © 2002 by The Haworth Press, Inc. All rights reserved.]*

KEYWORDS. Small business, education, action learning, industry-university cooperation, Slovenia

Miroslav Rebernik is Professor of Business Economics and Entrepreneurship, Head of Entrepreneurship Studies, Director of Institute for Entrepreneurship and Small Business Management, Faculty of Economics and Business at the University of Maribor, Razlagova 14, 2000 Maribor, Slovenia (E-mail: rebernik@uni-mb.si).

[Haworth co-indexing entry note]: "Companies as Business Laboratories." Rebernik, Miroslav. Co-published simultaneously in *Journal of Teaching in International Business* (International Business Press, an imprint of The Haworth Press, Inc.) Vol. 13, No. 3/4, 2002, pp. 99-114; and: *International Business Teaching in Eastern and Central European Countries* (ed: George Tesar) International Business Press, an imprint of The Haworth Press, Inc., 2002, pp. 99-114. Single or multiple copies of this article are available for a fee from The Haworth Document Delivery Service [1-800-HAWORTH 9:00 a.m. - 5:00 p.m. (EST). E-mail address: getinfo@haworthpressinc.com].

INTRODUCTION

Small and medium-sized companies constitute an important part of national economies all over the world. In spite of this, business and management schools don't consider them important enough to tailor curricula to their needs. The most relevant type of education to prepare one to enter the business world is entrepreneurship education, which is expanding rapidly, not only in the United States (Vesper 1993), but also in Europe (Landstroem, Veciana and Frank 1997). Several common characteristics should be taken into account when considering entrepreneurship education. First, as defined by Vesper (in Block and Stumpf 1993: 28), there are numerous types of entrepreneurs: business starters, intraprenenurs, self-employed individuals, acquirers, operators, deal makers, brokers and turnaround specialists. But as can be concluded from an overview of many entrepreneurship courses and programs, entrepreneurship education is still primarily tailored to business starters and maybe partially to intrapreneurs. Second, although the types of entrepreneurial jobs that students majoring in entrepreneurship and management programs are expected to perform, are numerous, all are tied to thorough knowledge about business and what it really means to run a business. As a rule, students do not learn much during their studies about what real life in companies is like. Somewhere down the road, business schools have forgotten that, as historians put it, "right up to the Second World War the academic content of business education was taken very much from business praxis" (Locke 1993: 64).

We do not lack papers that empirically and/or theoretically deal with the problems of business education (many such papers can be found in the *Journal of Teaching in International Business* and in the *Journal of Management Education*) or entrepreneurship education (e.g., Gorman, Hanlon and King 1997). What is missing are practical educational experiments which show that innovative ways can be devised within the current university system to prepare students for the challenges of work in small business environments. This paper will describe such an experiment.

GETTING A DRIVER'S LICENSE
WITHOUT DRIVING EXPERIENCE

The rapidly changing business environment characterized by the enlarged role of small and medium-sized companies, the globalization of business, information intensity and growing uncertainty has increased the value of human capital engaged in production, and has made traditional educational approaches for work in smaller companies unproductive. New methods of teaching people who will work in such an environment must be found.

Small business is not a shrunken form of big business. Individual management functions in smaller companies cannot be specialized to the same extent as those of large companies. In general, the educational process at universities does not take into account these important differences. Instead, it is oriented to the needs of big companies and educates specialists in fields such as marketing, finance, accounting, etc. But small business cannot afford specialists. It needs highly competent, practical individuals capable of handling a broad array of business problems.

The majority of university programs train people only to be employed and to work for others, and do not train them to be self-reliant owners and entrepreneurs, or to be able to undertake their own business career. In the majority of business programs throughout the world, students must wait until their graduation and the beginning of their business career to get first hand experience managing a company. Consider the implications of non-business schools educating their students in the same manner. There would probably be drivers who had never driven a car, doctors who had never dealt with a patient, architects who had never drawn a blueprint and painters who had never painted a picture.

BUSINESS EDUCATION: A JOINT TASK OF ACADEMICIANS, ENTREPRENEURS AND MANAGERS

The Faculty of Economics and Business at the University of Maribor in Slovenia operates an undergraduate Small Business Management program, an important aspect of which provides students' with practical work in companies. The program allows students to spend two days a week at the University and two days a week in companies over a course of four semesters, i.e. about 1,000 hours during a two-year period. Entrepreneurs and small business managers train students, and students (with the help of university academicians) solve real-world business problems. The program merges the talents of academicians and managers toward the same objective: effective business education and training which is relevant to the changed business environment.

The underlying philosophy of this innovative program, which started 8 years ago, is that education and training for people who will become either independent entrepreneurs, employees in a smaller company, or the owners and operators of smaller companies, must be different from the education and training given to individuals who will work for big companies. It must take into account at least three elements that exist in a small business: de-specialization of job tasks, resource poverty, and self-employment.

This program was designed and initiated through the cooperation of the following institutions of higher education: the University College of Boras (Sweden), the School of Economics and Commercial Law at the University of Gothenburg (Sweden), the De Vlerick School of Management at the University of Gent (Belgium), the Faculty of Economics and Banking at the University of Udine (Italy), and the Faculty of Economics and Business at the University of Maribor (Slovenia). Needed financial support was obtained from funds provided by the European Union (PHARE–TEMPUS), the Swedish Government, the Maribor Commune, and from tuition paid by mentoring companies.

THE AIMS AND CURRICULUM OF THE PROGRAM

The basic aim of this program is to produce graduates who can run and manage small and medium-sized companies or undertake other entrepreneurial jobs immediately after graduation, without needing a lengthy period to adjust to the business and to become acquainted with actual enterprise life.

After successfully completing their first two years of basic business economics studies, students can request admission to the small business management program. Upon admission, each qualified student is assigned to an appropriate smaller company, which meets certain pre-set criteria, and is capable of and willing to cooperate with the Faculty of Business and Economics to provide pertinent business education and training. Under the mentorship of the entrepreneur or the top manager of such a company during their course of study, the students validate their theoretical knowledge in these companies and obtain practical business skills.

The program consists of fourteen subjects (as shown in Table 1), which total 1,440 credit hours. Half of the credit hours are earned in a mentoring company where students work and do project work for each of their subjects.

TABLE 1. Obligatory Subjects in the Program for Management of Smaller Companies

	18 subjects completed during the first two years of studies	1,400 hrs.
	SUBJECTS TO BE COMPLETED IN THE SBM PROGRAM	HOURS
1.	Small Business Management	90
2.	Small Business Informatics	60
3.	Management Accounting	120
4.	Innovation Management	120
5.	Foreign Language III	60
6.	Operation Management	120
7.	Marketing for Small Business	120
8.	Financial Management	120
9.	Human Resource Management	120
10.	Company Law	120
11.	Project Management	120
12.	Quality Management	60
13.	Business Policy and Management	120
14.	Entrepreneurship	90
	TOTAL CREDIT HOURS	1,440

Students must pass evaluations in all subject areas. Every evaluation is divided into two parts: (1) a written and/or an oral exam, and (2) project work which seeks to solve a practical (real) problem in the mentoring company. While the exam, either written or oral, is taken individually, the project work concludes with a presentation in a seminar where other students and often entrepreneurs and managers comprise the audience. While the teacher of a subject is the only assessor of the first part of the examination, his/her assessment of the project work takes into consideration the presentation and discussion in the seminar, as well as the grade given by student's mentor at the company. The program ends with a dissertation, which provides a theoretical basis for the student's work and describes its application to a concrete project in a mentoring company.

COMPANIES AS BUSINESS LABORATORIES

A highly important part of the program is the students' practical work in companies. Each student is assigned to a small company, which usually has not less than 10 or more than 150 employees. Ideally, the company should perform as many different functions (production, accounting, marketing, finance, etc.) as possible, as it is important for the student to experience the greatest possible scope of tasks. The company should be "open," for in order to perform their tasks professionally and competently, students need access to all kinds of information. A student should be treated in the same way as any other reliable employee.

While performing its business operations, the company should pay respect to seriousness and its own reputation. It should avoid "moonlighting" and transactions of dubious value, which can challenge the integrity of students, reflect badly on the University, and undermine the activities intended to promote business education.

The company should not regard the student as a contract-based employee who performs routine tasks. The student must be viewed as a resource to the company. Students, on the other hand, are expected to play an active role in the company's operations and not just be observers. This does not imply that the performance of routine tasks is not desirable, but that they should not be a dominating activity.

It is important for the company to maintain a climate that is open to learning and change, thereby allowing student to contribute to the increased ability of the company. This is also important with regard to the reports made and the results achieved by the student. One of the conditions for selection of a mentoring company is that it provides the student with motivating feedback about the quality of his/her work.

The terms of the relationship among the mentoring company, the student and the university are specified in a formal, signed agreement among the three parties. In order to protect the companies and their business interests, students must refrain from discussing the company's internal affairs outside the study group of the students and teachers involved in the program. It is advantageous if companies that participate in the program belong to different branches of industry, trade and service activities.

The company is not obliged to pay the student for his/her work. However, each mentoring company pays $500 to the Faculty of Economics and Business. As compensation for this contribution, the company can expect quality work from a student unburdened by personal bias, the results of his/her seminar work which are aimed at solving specific problems within the company, and–through the student–the professional expertise of university instructors who are responsible for particular courses within the program.

Because the student, during his/her stay in the company, strives to conduct profound analytical investigations, we try to avoid using the same company for a student placement in succeeding years. Another student is thus given an opportunity to start anew. Such an approach also has larger benefits for the company.

DESIRED PEDAGOGICAL OUTCOMES

Roughly speaking, the pedagogical goal of the program is to familiarize students with the type of institution they are likely to work for after graduation. Since on a general level, all companies perform similar generic functions and follow similar missions, it is not of great importance what a company does, where is it located, etc., for learning to occur. For different students to get similar experience, they do not need to be placed in the same company. Since each student obtains his/her experience from different companies, there occur as many different and, at the same time, similar experiences as there are students in the program. Individual experience is enriched through a collective experience. We believe that students definitely learn what real-life is like in a company.

One of the most beneficial pedagodical outcomes of the "sandwiched" placement of students in a company for two years is that they cease fearing the unknown. The unknown is very often quite banal, but very real for those facing it. There are many things that worry students going to a company for the first time: how to talk to customers, how to ask questions, how to address the people around them, how to ask for help when needed; even how to answer a phone call. By the end of the program, students are much more self-confident and self-assured, for together with extensive theoretical and practical knowledge, they acquire some useful business etiquette.

Another valuable pedagogical outcome is that students lose their fear of raising questions or inquiring about things they are interested in. When, in the company, they are faced with a task they have to perform and are unsure how to do it, they are forced to seek help. No theoretizing helps when a mundane task, like sending an offer, charging a customer, or setting up an account must be performed. Tasks of this sort compel students to ask practical questions, which leads to a loss of the fear of questioning, a major impediment to learning. Not only do they learn to ask for help when they do not know how to perform a task, they also learn to ask a question which leads to the solution of their problem.

At least once a year, we meet with the school's alumni at a social gathering. Discussions with former students have revealed that after graduation some of them still did not know what they wanted to do for a living. However, their unanimous conclusion was that the program at least helped them to be sure about what they didn't want to do or become in their lives. After spending two years in a company, their perception of the real-world became much more realistic.

FACILITATING EXPOSURE TO A COMPANY

Exposure to a company is facilitated by the instructional components the students receive within each course. Because the courses in the program do not run parallel but consecutively in 5 or 6 weeks blocks, it is easier to give students exact instructions on what they are supposed to do in a company through the lectures in a particular course.

How it is all done? The program starts with a course on *Small Business Management* where students have to make a kind of SWOT analysis of all the business functions in the company. Instructions on performing the analysis are very detailed, with numerous illustrations, to make the students' first steps in the company easier. The instructions force students to talk to many people in the company in order to obtain information, and in doing so, to gain quick insight into what is happening in the company. The results of this initial analysis are sometimes not very useful to the company, but they produce other benefits. Students become well acquainted with the company and the people in it at the beginning of their association with it, and the people in the company learn that there is a student among them. In addition, the entrepreneur or lead manager gets a fresh perspective about the company, even if it is considered a little naive.

The next course in the program is *Small Business Informatics* where students again receive detailed instructions on how to scan the informational needs of the company. Instructions for the other courses in the program are less detailed and more is left unexplained. At the beginning of the lectures in the course, students do not get detailed instructions on what they must do in the company, but rather a detailed description of the syllabus and guidelines on how to prepare their seminar work. The methodology of preparing seminar work is explained at great length, but the content of such work is left open and undefined. The topic of the seminar work will result from a discussion between the student and his/her mentor in the company. The mentor will present a company problem to the student and he/she will try to solve it via the seminar process where he/she can benefit from a professor's expertise.

RECRUITING COMPANIES AND MATCHING
THEM WITH STUDENTS

What our students do in companies is not what is usually considered a typical student internship. Their experience embodies a whole array of activities that occur in the mentoring company. Not every student faces the same problems because students must cooperate with employees and cope with the same practical problems they deal with. To prevent students from getting too deeply involved and overloaded with mundane activities, an agreement is made with companies that only half of the student's time will be devoted to participating in the daily activities of the company, while the student will devote the rest of his/her time to his/her seminar work.

The selection of an appropriate mentoring company and mentor is very important. A company must perform enough activities for meaningful student involvement and face enough problems whose solution requires a slightly more theoretical basis. The mentor in the company must be able to assign students meaningful tasks and supply them out with everything they need to perform practical activities and prepare a seminar work product that will satisfy university standards, while solving a real company problem. Because the student will stay in the same mentoring company for two years, yet have no obligation to be employed by it after graduation, this is not a typical internship experience.

Companies are recruited and retained in three basic ways. The first way is by using the university's database of potential mentoring companies. Entries to the database are based on personal evaluations of the companies, the recommendations of colleagues and of the entrepreneurs we cooperate with, a company's goodwill as exhibited in the media, etc. The second way is to let students find a mentoring company on their own. The third way is for companies to come to us with a request to be included in the program. Irrespective of the mode, the same procedure is applied. We gather as much information as needed to determine the adequacy of the company, we talk with the entrepreneur, and we very often visit the company before making a decision.

We refrain from keeping the same company for more than two years. We like to engage it again later, but at least a year must pass in between. Some exceptions are made with companies that are very dynamic and very enthusiastic about keeping students all the time.

To match students and companies, we hold a series of meetings. The first one is held in mid-March, when second year students must communicate their intentions about participation in the study program during their third and fourth years of school. At the Faculty of Economics and Business, they can choose any one of seven programs: Finance and Banking, Marketing, Accounting and Auditing, General Management, International Trade, Economics and Small Business Management. Out of 250 students in the second year of study, typically about 40 of them express their intention to enroll in the Small Business Management program. With these students, we schedule a second meeting which is attended by some third and fourth year Small Business Management students, some professors and sometimes one or more mentors from the participating companies. The meeting involves a group discussion and clarification of the details of participation in the program. The organized part of the meeting usually lasts an hour, after which the professors and mentors leave the room so the students can talk with each other freely without being inhibited by the presence of others.

The next meeting is held in mid-June, by the end of summer exam period. At this meeting we ascertain the preferences of each student for a particular mentoring company. We make no in-depth measurement of student profiles, but ask simple questions like: "What are your special skills?" "What hobbies do you pursue?" "What courses in your studies have you up to now liked the most?" "Which have you disliked the most?" "What type of company would you like to work for?" "In what type of firm do you not want to be?" The aim of the interviews is to avoid mistakes in placing students. It is impossible to make a perfect match, but we can at least minimize possible conflicts, like placing a student who hates accounting in an auditing firm or placing a vegetarian in a butcher's shop.

We encourage students to go out in the field and to find a company by themselves. We also give them a list of good companies and allow them to make their own arrangements. In both instances, we provide them with an official letter signed by the Chair of Small Business Management studies to give them the necessary authority for discussions with the entrepreneur or lead manager of a company. But as mentioned earlier, we always make the final selection.

The final selection of students and their matching companies is made in mid-September, two weeks before the beginning of the fall term in October. On their first visit to the company, the students take with them an Agreement of Cooperation which must be signed by the student, a representative of the Faculty of Economics and Business and a representative of the company. The Agreement stipulates, among other provisions, that cooperation among the three parties can be terminated at any time if any of the parties thinks cooperation is no longer feasible.

Fortunately, the termination of such agreements happens very rarely. In eight years, we have had only four such cases.

ACTION LEARNING OR REAL-WORLD LEARNING

The Revans Center for Action Learning and Research at the University of Salford defines action learning as "a process of inquiry, beginning with the experience of not knowing what to do next, and finding that an answer is not available from current expertise." (Powell 1999).

Action learning as originally developed by Reg Revans in the 1940's proved to be a good way to educate managers, particularly those with high levels of responsibility but a long absence from higher education (O'Hara, Weber and Reeve 1996). It is also suitable for MBA programs where it can be highly successful (Dilworth 1996). Many examples of successful corporate education in companies such as Phillips, Dutch Royal, Shell Group, Motorola, Unilever, and Daimler-Benz AG (Ready 1995) show the effectiveness of an action learning approach regardless of whether it is used in an original or an adapted form. What we do in the Small Business Management program is far from the equivalent of Operation Centurion (Ready 1995), in which Jan Timmer introduced more than 20 action learning projects that successfully restructured Phillips. The majority of action learning projects are authentic followers of Revan's generic idea of the education of management (Parkes 1998). Our program was never designed as an action learning process, although it contains some action learning components.

Although our program is not an example of *action learning*, we can still use Revan's formula $L = P + Q$. Experience is translated to learning through seminar projects in which students have to combine the programmed knowledge (P) acquired in the classroom. In order to solve certain problems they encounter in the company in which they are working they must mix the programmed knowledge with questions (Q). Since in the beginning students receive detailed instructions on how to undertake questioning in the company, we can modify Revan's formula a little, as follows: $L = P + Q + PQ$ (i.e., learning (L) is equal to programmed knowledge (P) plus spontaneous questioning (Q) plus programmed questioning (PQ). In this educational model, the main role of the faculty is to provide programmed knowledge and to help students to adequately solve the company problem which was selected for seminar work. The company mentor assists the student to freely ask questions and paves the way for him/her to obtain the information needed to fulfill his/her assigned tasks.

Is our program an action learning model? We don't think so. We do not form learning teams as "sets." Students do not have the right to take action, at least not during the first half of their stay in the company. There is no tutorial session in the company, etc. Also, other elements are missing from our program that are "prescribed" in an action learning model of education, such as peer evaluation of one's performance, reciprocation of advice and criticism, analysis of learning results, participant feedback, etc. (Revans 1983, 1984).

If we embrace a dichotomy of management education between the professional education model and the action learning model, our Small Business Management program falls somewhere between the two. We think it is more appropriate to view it as a real-world learning model (Bilimoria 1998). It should also not be regarded as experiential learning. We do not place students in simulated, fictitous organizations, but in actual, functioning companies with all their complexities and all large and small problems that must be solved on a daily basis.

THE INTERNATIONAL COMPONENT OF THE PROGRAM

Slovenia is a small country with 2 million inhabitants, 600,000 employees and a little over 100,000 companies. Being so small, it is almost impossible to teach any business subject without taking into account the international environment in which Slovene businesses operate. In addition to the international context in which subjects are taught, students are exposed to guest teachers from abroad, and to their international experience. Cases presented in class are normally not about Slovenia per se, and are delivered in English.

With the money paid by mentoring companies and the money earned from students' business activities, we organize student study trips to companies and to SME supporting institutions abroad. In five years we have visited some 30 companies and business supporting institutions in Sweden, Belgium, the Netherlands, Germany, Italy, Austria and the USA. So each generation of business students is directly exposed to the international business scene. Their experience is afterward published in a journal, *Bilten MMP* that is delivered without charge to all students in the program, as well as to mentoring companies, professors and sponsors. For the time being, we don't have mentoring companies from other countries, although some of the students in the Small Business

Management program previously finished a semester or a full year at a foreign university and, while doing so, obtained some experience working for a foreign company.

MANAGEMENT ISSUES

One of the main challenges and dilemmas of the program is that it is very time consuming for everyone involved. The success of the program is dependent on the willingness of the program leader to be constantly available, not only to invest his time in organizing and leading the program, but also in promoting it among entrepreneurs. The program is also heavily dependent on the expertise of the professors teaching in the program, as they are constantly under the vigilant eyes of the business people and students. Working for a state university, their additional efforts are not rewarded monetarily, so it can be hard to maintain their enthusiasm. To run such a program, additional funds are needed which are provided by the mentoring companies. Because their money is involved, companies insist on securing good students and on seminar activities that are of real, practical value for the company.

In operating the program, we face many of the problems Bilimoria (1998) writes about: instructors' evaluation and rewards, compensation for time spent mentoring and consulting, etc. In addition, not every instructor is capable of real-world learning technology. Not only must instructors be good, experienced educators, they also must have enough credibility to discuss practical problems with students and, if necessary, with the mentors in the company. In our model where companies serve as entrepreneurship laboratories, not only does learning move out of the classroom into the real world, the professors have to move along, too. For such a paradigmatic shift in education, it is not enough that only one course is run this way, the whole university-industry relationship needs to be redesigned. The earlier model, where the university is a provider of educational services and industry is a buyer, is evolving into a new model where industry and the university are partners in pursuit of the same "product"–well educated, trained and practice-effective graduates.

RESULTS AND LESSONS LEARNED

In eight years of running the Small Business Management program at the University of Maribor, we have developed strong relations with many entrepreneurs and the owners and managers of small and medium-sized companies. Students have finished over 500 projects in mentoring companies. Some fifty entrepreneurs and managers have participated in classroom discussions.

One of the very positive outcomes of running the small business program has been recognition of the need for small business management education involving both academia and entrepreneurs and managers. While striving for cooperation between small companies and the university, we have encountered two noteworthy mindsets. With respect to the business community, the majority of entrepreneurs and managers in smaller companies have felt that cooperating with the university in this manner was, from a practical point of view, a waste of time. Not without its own biases, academia has revealed deeply ingrained beliefs that anything practical should not be given credence by the university, because it is not scientific. Through running the program we have succeeded in debunking many of these false pictures of reality. Today we see evidence of changed mindsets or shifts in attitudes on the part of both academics and entrepreneurs and managers (Rebernik 1994, 2000). Professors are now more deeply involved in authentic business practices and are acquiring deeper insight into business problems and the learning needs of SMEs. Very often, students succeed in opening the eyes of entrepreneurs and getting them to think about what their business "needs to know, what it needs to learn, how it might learn it, and who from" (Gibb 1997: 20).

We have learned that in such an educational venture, to sustain the success of entrepreneurship and small business management education at the university level, three partners are of equal importance: students, teachers and companies (Figure 1).

Teachers must be able to perform consulting services for entrepreneurs, if asked, and must possess mentoring abilities to advise students, when needed. They must be directly involved with business, and be experienced on international scale.

Not every student meets the requirements for combining academic studies with managerial practice, no matter how bright or hardworking she or he may be. Besides satisfying certain formal requirements such as high grades and language skills, an appropriate personality, ingenuity, and communication and cooperation skills are also needed, to make sure that both the student and the company will benefit from this experience.

Finally, entrepreneurs/managers and companies have to be carefully selected. Managers are of particularly crucial importance. Without their commitment to cooperate with the university and to take part in the educational and training process, the management program, no matter how

FIGURE 1. Partners in Effective Business Education

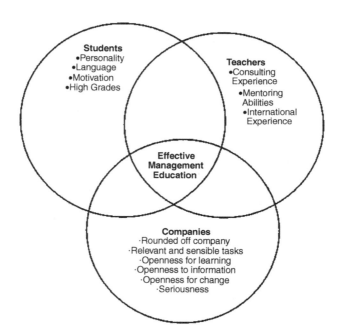

well organized, would just be an ordinary university program, "just another brick in the wall." With the commitment of entrepreneurs and managers, the companies play for small business management and entrepreneurship students a role similar to that which laboratories play for chemistry students and flight simulators play for future pilots.

REFERENCES

Bilimoria, D. (1998). From Classroom Experience to Real-World Learning: A Diasporic Shift in Management Education. *Journal of Management Education*, Vol. 22, No. 3.

Block, Z., & Stumpf, S. (1993). "Entrepreneurship Education Research: Experience and Challenge." *In The State of the Art of Entrepreneurship* edited by Sexton, Donald and Kasarda, John. Boston: PWS-Kent.

Dilworth, R. (1996). "Action Learning: Bridging Academic and Workplace Domains. Employee Counselling Today." *The Journal of Workplace Learning*. 8, 6, 45-53.

Gibb, A. (1997). "Small Firm's Training and Competitiveness: Building Upon the Small Business as a Learning Organization," *International Small Business Journal*, 15, 3, 13-29.

Gorman, G., & Hanlon, D., & King, W. (1997). "Some Research Perspectives on Entrepreneurship Education, Enterprise Education and Education for Small Business Management: A Ten-year Literature Review." *International Small Business Journal*. 15, 3, 56-77.

Landstroem, H., & Frank, H., & Veciana, J. (Eds). (1997). *Entrepreneurship and Small Business Research in Europe: An ECSB Survey*. Aldershot: Avebury.

Locke, R. (1993). Education and Entrepreneurship: An Historian's View. In *Entrepreneurship, Networks and Modern Business*, edited by Brown, J. and Rose, M. Manchester: Manchester University Press.

O'Hara, S., & Webber, T., & Reeve, S. (1996). "Action Learning in Management Education." *Education + Learning*, 38, 8, 16-21.

Parkes, D. (1998). "Action Learning: Business Applications in North America. *Journal of Workplace Learning*. Vol 10, No. 3, pp.165-168.

Powell, J. et al. (1999). *Action Learning for Innovation and Construction. Problems of Participation and Connection Conference*. Amsterdam, April 6-9, 1999.

Ready, D. (1995). "Educating the Survivors." *The Journal of Business Strategy*. 16, 2, Mar/Apr 1995.

Rebernik, M. (1994). "Mental Models as the Pivot of the West-East Knowledge Transfer." *In Small Business Management in The New Europe* edited by Gibb, A. and Rebernik, M. Maribor: EIM.

Rebernik, M., Mulej, M. (2000). "Requisite Holism, Isolating Mechanisms and Entrepreneurship." *Kybernetes*. 29, 9/10, 1126-1140.

Revans, R. (1983). "Action Learning: Its Terms and Character." *Management Decision*. 21, 1, 39-51.

Revans, R. (1984). "Action Learning: Are We Getting There?" *Management Decision*, 22, 1, 45-53.

Vesper, K., & Gartner, W. (1997. "Measuring Progress in Entrepreneurship Education." *Journal of Business Venturing*, 12, 5, 403-421.

Vesper, Karl. 1993. *Entrepreneurship Education 1993*. Los Angeles: The Anderson School, UCLA.

The Role of Networking in the Creation of Local Management Knowledge: The Case of the Republic of Moldova

Mihaela Kelemen
Gordon Pearson
Paul Forrester
John Hassard
Valentin Railean
Rodica Hincu

SUMMARY. This paper analyses the role of networking in the creation of local management knowledge in the Republic of Moldova. At the outset, the paper sketches the economic and political context of this Eastern European country that has recently gained its independence from the Soviet Union. In so doing, the paper highlights the importance accorded to

Mihaela Kelemen is affiliated with the Department of Management & European Research Centre, Keele University, Staffordshire, ST5 5BG, UK (E-mail: m.l.kelemen @keele.ac.uk), Gordon Pearson is affiliated with the Department of Management, Keele University, Staffordshire, ST5 5BG, UK (E-mail: g.j.pearson@keele.ac.uk), Paul Forrester is affiliated with Aston Business School, Aston University, Birmingham, B4 7ET, UK (E-mail: p.l.forrester@aston.ac.uk), John Hassard is affiliated with Manchester School of Management, UMIST, PO Box 88, Manchester, M60 1QD (E-mail: john.hassard@umist.ac.uk), Valentin Railean is affiliated with The International Institute of Management (IMI), Str Hristo Botev 9/1, Christina, Moldova, MD 2043, and Rodica Hincu is affiliated with The International Institute of Management (IMI), Str Hristo Botev 9/1, Christina, Moldova, MD 2043.

[Haworth co-indexing entry note]: "The Role of Networking in the Creation of Local Management Knowledge: The Case of the Republic of Moldova." Kelemen, Mihaela et al. Co-published simultaneously in *Journal of Teaching in International Business* (International Business Press, an imprint of The Haworth Press, Inc.) Vol. 13, No. 3/4, 2002, pp. 115-132; and: *International Business Teaching in Eastern and Central European Countries* (ed: George Tesar) International Business Press, an imprint of The Haworth Press, Inc., 2002, pp. 115-132. Single or multiple copies of this article are available for a fee from The Haworth Document Delivery Service [1-800-HAWORTH 9:00 a.m. - 5:00 p.m. (EST). E-mail address: getinfo@haworthpressinc.com].

reforming management education in the successful transition to a market economy. Four models of reforming management education are then outlined and it is suggested that the networking model is the most viable for the Moldavian context. Having accounted for their involvement with the Moldavian International Institute of Management (IMI), the authors proceed to discuss the aims and objectives of the very first indigenous MBA programme developed by the Institute. While the "management of obstacles" at both macro and micro level has been an arduous task, IMI has emerged successfully out of this task due to the networking approach adopted in the construction of local management knowledge. Its entrepreneurial orientation helped IMI to proactively engage in local and international partnerships with businesses, government bodies, universities, and charitable foundations, a process which facilitated the creation of a network whose long-term survival and central role to reforming management education in Moldova is unquestionable. *[Article copies available for a fee from The Haworth Document Delivery Service: 1-800-HAWORTH. E-mail address: <getinfo@haworthpressinc.com> Website: <http://www. HaworthPress.com> © 2002 by The Haworth Press, Inc. All rights reserved.]*

KEYWORDS. Moldava, networking, management education, management knowledge

INTRODUCTION

Since the fall of communism, management education has been regarded as key to the successful transition from planned to market economy in Eastern Europe. The reform of management education has been a process fraught with difficulties. The paper sheds light on the achievements and difficulties with this process in the Republic of Moldova, a small Eastern European country which has not only freed itself from communism but also from the tentacles of the Soviet "empire."

We start by providing a synopsis of the Moldavian economy which is the background against which we discuss the development of a local management education model. The model has been developed by the International Institute of Management (IMI) from Christina, becoming operational in September, 1998. The success of the model lies in the networking approach adopted by IMI, an approach which stresses the active role of the local institute in the creation of local management knowledge via a dynamic and effective participation into partnerships with local businesses, government agencies as well as foreign institutions and foundations.

Consideration has been given to the possibility of developing a theoretical framework of such networking that might be pertinent to local knowledge creation particularly in other ex Soviet situations. However, the Moldavian economy and industry are different from those of other Eastern European states of which the authors have direct experience and theory development based on this grounding would appear to have limited potential for generalization. Nevertheless, the insights gained in Moldova could make a distinctive contribution to a more general model.

SETTING THE BACKGROUND: THE REPUBLIC OF MOLDOVA

The Republic of Moldova is situated in Eastern Europe bordering the Ukraine and Romania. It has a population of 4.4m people with a mixed ethnic background: Moldavians/Romanians represent 64.5%, Ukrainian and Russian nationals make up 26%, while the rest of the population is made of Gagauz, Jewish, Bulgarian and other nationalities. The predominant religion is Eastern Orthodox and the official language is Moldavian (virtually, the same as the Romanian language). Like the majority of former Soviet and Soviet-satellite countries in Eastern Europe, the Republic of Moldova is undergoing a major transition from a centralized command economy to a more decentralized market economy. In what follows we outline briefly the achievements and failure of the transitional process and the impact this has had upon management education.

The Moldavian economy relies heavily on agriculture, featuring fruits, vegetables, wine and tobacco. Its main industries are food processing, agricultural machinery, foundry equipment and textiles. The country has no mineral deposits and is highly dependent on Russia for nearly all oil, gasoline and coal. The country's most important trade partners are Russia and Romania.

There have been two phases in the transition process in Moldova. The first phase (1993-1996) appears to have been rather successful particularly in terms of inflation suppression, national currency stabilization, the beginning of mass privatization, and the commencement of industrial enterprises restructuring. The second phase (1997 to date) appears to have been less successful. It has relied heavily on administrative methods applied by the Government (pressures on tax collection, sale of jet-fighters, etc.), but has only enjoyed weak legal support from the Parliament. Its failure has been attributed mainly to accrued domestic structural flaws including a lack of structural changes at the micro-economic level, weaknesses in the state management system and, after autumn 1998, the Russian financial crisis. According to local and foreign experts, the main reason for poor economic performance was a power vacuum in the country resulting in disunity between the President, Parliament and Government. The non-enforcement of laws was evident, corruption of state structures was rife and a considerable part of the economy became a "shadow economy".

The Moldavian government approach to ensuring macro-economic stability relied heavily on a strict monetary policy. However, despite some positive results in the first transitional phase, it became clear that the economy was not being steered in the right direction. For example, in 1998 the GDP was three times lower than in 1990 with the result that Moldova had the lowest GDP per capita amongst all other CIS countries, representing US$454 in 1998. Furthermore, the inefficient legal regulation of various aspects of the economic life in conjunction with unreformed state machinery encouraged the emergence of corruption and organized crime. This hindered the harmonious development of the private business sector. The "shadow economy" developed fast. Its share as compared to the formal economy grew from 25% in 1992 to 40% in 1994 and 55-60% in 1998. Furthermore, tax evasion increased over that period from 3% of the consolidated budget income to 25%. These phenomena have had significant adverse effects on living standards. Statistical data reveal a dramatic decline in people's welfare. The real monthly disposable income per person has dropped by 11% and reached its lowest level in the last four years of 118 lei ($14).[1]

Moldova has many of the features of a liberal economy, notably in terms of political openness and the existence of laws aiming to serve the transition. However, there are few mechanisms in place to ensure law enforcement, corruption is rife and the shadow economy threatens to take over the formal economy. Consequently overall confidence is low. Amidst all these problems, reforming the mindset of the country's managers appears a daunting task. Yet, management education is regarded as essential in ensuring the success of the transition to a market economy, and the development of the first indigenous MBA in 1998, by the International Institute of Management (IMI) is indicative of the country's determination to succeed.

APPROACHES TO REFORMING MANAGEMENT EDUCATION IN EASTERN EUROPE

Despite the premium placed on the need to develop managers with skills and competencies aligned to the demands of the transition to a market economy (Kelemen, 1999), there are no immediate successful recipes as to how to reform management education in the countries of Eastern Europe. A number of approaches have been discussed in the literature, namely the laissez-faire, the government control, the foreign domination and the networking approach (cf. Kozminski, 1996) but there is insufficient empirical evidence regarding their viability and potential for success. In what follows we review their advantages and disadvantages and provide evidence from the Moldavian setting to support the claim that the networking approach is an effective strategy for creating and disseminating management knowledge in Eastern Europe.

The laissez faire approach endorses the view that the present state of affairs should be allowed to continue in the hope that market forces will eventually eliminate weaker institutions and poor-quality programmes. This approach may sound attractive, partly because there is a certain phobia regarding government intervention and partly because of the existing budget deficits and resultant cuts in spending on education. However, the economies of Eastern Europe have not yet fully adjusted to market economy principles; recession continues, there is a lack of institutional support and information is far from perfect. Under these circumstances it is apparent that management education and development will continue to fragment into a large number of weak institutions and programmes. Thus the laissez faire approach appears simply to be nonviable; intervention will be necessary if these unhappy results are to be avoided.

At the other end of the spectrum, the government control approach involves substantial intervention. For this to be effective would require a clear vision of the desired system supported by detailed planning and allocation of resources. It is unlikely that Eastern European countries will favour this approach partly because of the weaknesses and instability of governments and partly because of lack of domestic resources. Furthermore, some may fear that the resulting management curricula would be too inward looking, reproducing knowledge practices grounded in the earlier, "socialist" paradigms and not accounting for the global and local changes that have affected these countries in the last ten years or so.

The foreign domination approach implies that foreign governments would establish and run a number of management development programmes in post-communist countries. This requires a great deal of political will and material resources from the international community and might come with various strings attached to it. Moreover, such an approach would involve the replication of Western MBA programmes and the imposition of Western theories of management at the expense of locally constructed systems of management knowledge. There is considerable and growing disquiet about such an approach, which is seen by some Eastern European recipients as condescending and patronizing (Gilbert, 2000). Controversy about Western models of education (O'Donoghue, 1994), and the criticisms levied upon Western models of knowledge in general (Harding, 1996), arising from the early days of economic transition, suggest the approach may well not achieve the intended result.

The networking approach requires some form of association between interested actors: business schools, universities, the business community, government agencies, foreign donors, professional agencies and so on. Such loosely-structured networks can enable interested parties to stay in touch and be informed about each other's activities, interests and problems. "The open-ended relational features of networks, with their relative absence of explicit "quid pro quo" behaviour, greatly enhance their ability to transmit and learn new knowledge and skills" (Powell, 1991, 272). The initiative to form and operate such networks should stay with the local institutions: Western partners should provide "assistance" and participate in common problem solving processes with the view to develop original, innovative solutions to management development in Eastern Europe (Kozminski, 1996). The success of the networking approach is illustrated by the case of IMI, the Moldavian institute which developed the first indigenous MBA as a result of forging relationships with various parties such as the government, local businesses, foreign agencies and universities.

THE IMI MBA PROGRAMME: A SHORT OVERVIEW

Keele University involvement with IMI started in 1998 when the British Council invited bids for grants aimed to help in reforming the education system in the ex-Soviet Union. IMI contacted Keele University via the British Council and after a preliminary visit paid by three Keele academics to Chisinau, the capital of the Republic of Moldova, it was agreed that a bid be made. The bid was successful and at the end of 1998, the collaboration between Keele and IMI started to take shape. The paper is based on data collected throughout the three visits to the UK by the Moldavian party and the four visits to Chisinau by the British party. During these visits, the authors have had formal and informal discussions with each other as well as other staff and numerous MBA students from Keele and IMI. This data was supplemented by participant observation and document examination: in particular, the authors have attended lectures and seminars offered on the IMI MBA programme and have analyzed the content of the modules created as a result of Keele/IMI cooperation. Given that the project leader is a fluent speaker of both English and Romanian and that all Moldavian professors had a good command of English, the data analysis and the writing of the paper unfolded without much difficulty.

The International Institute of Management (IMI) from Christina is closely associated with the State University from Moldova, the equivalent of a university postgraduate business school in UK, charged with offering MBA-type management courses. The first Moldavian MBA became fully operational in September 1998 as a result of Mimi's co-operation with a number of foreign foundations such as Sores and Eurasia and their active participation in partnerships with local businesses, government agencies, as well as foreign partnerships such as The Technical Assistance to the Commonwealth of Independent States (TACIS) and the Regional Academic Partnership Scheme REAP. Although it is difficult to assess the contribution of each individual collaboration to the development of the MBA, we believe that the REAP partnership has been instrumental in finalizing the plans for, and the successful launch of, the MBA programme, and provided a most fertile ground for the creation and dissemination of local management knowledge.

The REAP partnership scheme started in 1997, being funded by the British Government's Department of International Development and administered, on their behalf, by the British Council. REAP brings together universities from the ex Soviet Union and the UK in an attempt to "strengthen the capacity of local higher education institutions to provide training to meet the socio-economic and political needs of the former Soviet Union countries" (REAP Project Logical Framework).

This paper focuses on the lessons learnt by IMI and its British counterpart, Keele University, as a result of their participation to the REAP partnership which started in February 1998 and is ongoing. The REAP partnership represented a coincidence of needs for both IMI and Keele University. Keele staff have a long-standing research interest in the management and social implications of the economic changes taking place in the transitional economies of Eastern Europe (Kelemen and Hristov, 1998; Kelemen, 1999). Previous research at Keele has focused mainly on the making of organizational and individual identities in countries such as Romania, Bulgaria, Estonia and the Czech Republic.

The Republic of Moldova with its unique economic and political situation represented a new challenge for Keele researchers. IMI, on the other hand, was looking for a UK partner to supplement their existing European links with the Universities of Grenoble, Genoa and Palma. At the time, IMI expressed an interest for the REAP partnership; they already had in place a clear plan regarding the development of an indigenous MBA.

Although the structure of the Moldavian MBA (See Table 1) is modelled to a great extent after that of Keele's MBA, the content of each module has been fully adapted to the Moldavian context. Both parties have worked closely to assess the needs of the Moldavian audience and develop modules, which would meet these needs. Rather than engaging in a unidirectional process of knowledge transfer which is typically based on the view that theories and models developed in the West are appropriate to all other cultural settings, Keele and IMI have engaged in a process of "mutual meaning creation" (Jankowicz, 1999), one that recognizes the importance of local voices in the conversation of management research and practice. Both parties have nurtured and respected each other's views and have built upon existing differences in order to enhance their own ability to learn and self-reflect.

TABLE 1. MBA Course Outline

Duration:	1 year part-time
Core Modules: (7 taken)	Financial Management Organisational Behaviour Management accounting Business Analysis and Research Methods International Commerce and Foreign Direct Investment Quality Management Strategic Management
Option Modules: (2 taken)	Business Ethics Marketing Information Technology & Systems Managing Financial Services
Dissertation	Work based primary research

The leading role in the development of the Moldavian MBA was taken by IMI staff who assumed full responsibility for the management and provision of the courses. For example, IMI staff has introduced new teaching and learning methods, among which the case study method, group exercises, video-sessions and empirical mini-research projects. The case study approach is the most popular teaching device on Western MBAs aiming to develop students' analytical, creative, communication and self-analysis skills (Thomas, 1996). As Western cases have become more widely available in Moldova, the need for indigenous cases has become more and more pressing. IMI staff have developed a collection of cases, which comment upon the success, and failures of Moldavian and international organizations operating in Moldova. A number of group exercises have also been designed in order to promote teamwork and improve problem solving and presentation skills among the students. As local educational video material is not as yet available in Moldova, staff have relied entirely on Western video material. Given that all students on the programme speak English fluently and that most of the issues at stake are global, students tend to find such material both relevant and insightful. Lastly, IMI staff have introduced an individual mini-project which involves collecting data first hand (through interviews, surveys and participant observation) on a particular hands-on topic within a local organizational setting, analyzing the data and reporting the findings back to the class.

In conjunction with these new teaching methods, a number of new assessment methods have been introduced, such as written assignments in the form of critical essays on particular topics and continuous assessment for group exercises and presentations. Given that IMI staff took a leading role in the development of the MBA, the withdrawal of Keele from the programme at the end of the REAP partnership will not pose any great difficulty to the programme's future sustainability.

While the achievements of IMI are remarkable, they have not been easy. IMI have had to handle and remove numerous macro- and micro-level obstacles. The "management of obstacles" is still ongoing, demanding clarity of objectives, determination and a strong belief in the long-term future of the MBA.

DEVELOPING THE MBA:
"THE MANAGEMENT OF OBSTACLES"

The single most important macro-level obstacle to the transition process in Moldova has been the chronic political instability. The numerous and unpredictable changes witnessed by the political scene have translated in inconsistent and changeable government policies, corruption and bureaucratic red tape. Interestingly enough, IMI has remained relatively untouched by the vicissitudes of the political life and the relatively slow process of economic transition. One of the reasons stems from the fact that the deepening of the economic crisis has triggered and legitimized the need for more and better-qualified managers who are capable of designing and implementing solutions to the crisis. Ironically, the worse the economic situation, the bigger the perceived need for managers and the higher the prestige and importance accorded to management. The political crisis has also not affected the success of the Institute in attracting students and in establishing connections with local businesses and government agencies. This may be due to the entrepreneurial orientation of the Institute's leadership and the fact that recent political and economic discourses in Moldova follow Western practice in celebrating "the enterprise" (OECD, 1998; Gorman et al., 1997) and view entrepreneurship as having a formidable role in achieving change and progress in the Moldavian economy and society.

As far as micro-level barriers are concerned, evidence from other eastern European countries suggests that there are at least four factors which could detract from the goal of developing and implementing relevant and successful management education models in Eastern Europe (Kozminski, 1996). These are:

1. *Institutional and cultural rigidity.* Although IMI is formally connected with the Moldavian State University, the connection is rather loose. IMI is funded through a number of international projects and its reliance upon state funds is rather limited. Consequently, IMI sets out its own objectives and decides upon the ways to go about implementing them. The Institute is capable of rapid development and adjustment of curricula without administrative interference by the State University and with considerable financial independence. For example, the Institute has set up its own course review committees and procedures. Every course is reviewed once a year by the review committee whose sole responsibility is to ensure that courses are up to date and reflect current economic issues. Furthermore, Mimi's culture is one of open communication and flexibility, a far cry from the bureaucratic culture of the State University. This culture is driven by Mimi's rector whose entrepreneurial qualities have been instrumental in establishing and managing existing partnerships (Kirzner, 1973) and in

attracting young and promising academics to the Institute. The rector (who is one of the authors of the paper) is well aware that in order to compete effectively in a constantly changing environment, leaders must provide meaning for their followers and that the most effective mechanism for doing so is the establishment and continuous re-enactment of a culture that respects and nurtures individual contributions (Peters and Austin, 1985).

2. *Inadequate human resources in universities.* Most higher education institutions from Eastern Europe have had difficulties in adjusting their organizational cultures to the requirements of the market. This was due to the high degree of inertia present in the system and the fact that the leadership of such institutions remained in the hands of the "old guard". Furthermore, new graduates found better work opportunities in business and consulting and fled from the meagre salaries offered by the public sector. Those remaining in state higher education were forced to augment their incomes by taking on extra teaching at the newly formed private Universities. IMI itself relies to some extent on staff employed by the State University but the core of its lecturers is independently hired. With salaries three times higher than the equivalent in the state university and opportunities to be (re)trained at Western institutions among which one can name Grenoble University, Palma University and Genoa University, staff morale is high and academic abilities and qualifications are comparable to Western counterparts. Thus local staff is more than capable to conduct research on management topics and employ state of art teaching methods. The authors of this paper have equally shared the writing of this paper and we suspect it is impossible to guess which parts are to be attributed to British authors and which parts are to be attributed to Moldavian academics, due to the latter's comparable research training and proficiency in English.

3. Inappropriate or lack of foreign know how. In the early stages of the transition to the market economy, Eastern European universities had little exposure to Western management theories and techniques. However, the situation has since been reversed to the extent that local ways of theorizing have, in some cases, been entirely replaced by Western forms of management thinking. Anything that resonated with socialist modes of thinking and organization was labelled "outdated" and "inappropriate." However, recent research suggests that managerial skills and knowledge acquired in the socialist regime are still highly relevant

to running the economy: informal negotiation with the government, playing politics and having friends and connections in the right place are as essential in the capitalist economy as they had been in the socialist one (Kelemen, 1999). Although IMI has been exposed to foreign managerial know-how from a very early stage, thanks to a number of research grants offered by the European Union (EU) and various foreign foundations, it had not become totally dependent on such know-how. IMI has used Western management knowledge and techniques in a reflexive and critical manner, retaining only those aspects that made sense to their particular setting and building on them to reflect local practice and zeitgeist.

4. *Lack of co-operation with the local business community.* Co-operation with the business community is essential for the creation of relevant management knowledge. However, a substantial gap between management theory and managerial practice in the West has been identified (Astley and Zammuto, 1992) and it might therefore seem unlikely that such Western theories would deliver appropriate understandings and solutions to the problems of Eastern European management practice. It is therefore important that local researchers and local businesses in Eastern Europe are engaged in a continuous dialogue. IMI has achieved this with distinction. It has enjoyed the support of the local business community since its inception. Such businesses have sent their managers on the course, granted research access to academics and students alike and provided feedback which enabled more adequate curriculum development and programme structuring. Mimi's rector has played a significant role in creating and sustaining such networks, thanks to his entrepreneurial qualities and the clarity of aims and objectives pursued by the Institute (Lachmann, 1986).

CONSTRUCTING LOCAL MANAGEMENT KNOWLEDGE THROUGH NETWORKING AND ACTIVE PARTICIPATION IN PARTNERSHIPS

Traditionally, knowledge transfer has been viewed as a one-way process in which the object of knowledge and the transmitter were the most important elements. Numerous Western consultants and academics have reinforced this model by upholding Western theories of management as universal panaceas for all contexts and settings. This is a common feature of much emergent management theory, representing a stage of theory development rather than ever being a valid approach in its own right.

However, there are no universal panaceas. One-way communication from West to East is no more likely to be effective than the old fashioned top-down communication of Fordism and scientific management. Out of its native context it will be unlikely to succeed. Whereas Fordism was a response to the previously unknown possibilities of mass production technologies, the native context of one-way West-East communications is the one Eastern managers recognized as condescending and patronizing. It therefore has no prospect of success.

The management problem itself changed quite radically since the days of Ford. In most situations it no longer concerned "how to get large numbers of relatively unskilled and uneducated people to do unpleasant work and do it efficiently in return for wages set low enough to make a sufficient profit," but "how to attract, retain and give opportunities to highly skilled and educated people working in smaller numbers with a high degree of autonomy and with their rates of pay no longer the main cost drivers." (Pearson, 1999, p. 4). This requires new and flexible approaches which are sensitive to the particular situation under consideration.

Top-down communication was replaced by an "uncritical acceptance of the efficacy of open communications" (Eisenberg & Witten, 1987, p418). But this was no panacea of organizational ills either. The idea of simple open organizations had emerged with the human relations school which saw it as an integrating mechanism between manager and employee (Mayo, 1945; Roethlisberger & Dickson, 1947). Some later writers recognized these approaches as having the managerialist aim of manipulating employees to increase their productivity. Later researchers emphasized the mutually supportive relationships of managers and employees which might be advanced through open communications (Likert, 1967). Eisenberg and Witten (1987, p. 423) propose a contingency perspective in which "communication strategies reflect individual goals and situational characteristics". The situational characteristics in the present context include the cultural boundaries across which communication takes place. It cannot simply be "opened," like some electromagnetic system which can be repackaged by a translator and switched on at the destination by turning a key (Kwiatkowski and Sanders, 1993).

More recently, models of communication recognize the paramount importance of the receiver in the communication process. Communication does not take place unless the receiver receives–the tree falling in the forest does so silently if there is no one there to hear it. The crucial element in knowledge transfer is the receiver of knowledge, not the sender. The receivers of the knowledge interpret knowledge through their own cultural and cognitive frames of reference, thus moulding and changing the object of knowledge in ways unintended by the producers and senders of knowledge.

The knowledge which is intended to be communicated passes through a process of coding by the sender and decoding by the receiver. The coding and decoding process may both be imperfect and both be shaped by local cultural factors in which the sender and receiver operate. Thus the knowledge which leaves the Western "experts" and passes through cultural filters, most importantly in this case, those which are local to the receiver, before becoming received knowledge. Kostera (1996) argues that knowledge that thus travels from the West to the East is subject to this creative friction between the two cultures and this friction provides new insights into how to manage successfully in the former Eastern bloc. Top-down West East communication cannot capture any of these benefits.

Communication in networks is, of course, more complex than this. It is not simply two way, passing through two cultural filters, but is multi-directional, with the potential for creating even more complex and productive frictions. The power of networks is demonstrated in famous multi-organizational networks such as Silicon Valley in California, Route 128 in Boston and the Thames Valley corridor in UK (Hastings, 1993). It has become commonplace that in today's global village with its fast developing technology, no organization can survive without engaging in technological collaborations, strategic alliances, joint ventures and networks (Child & Faulkner, 1998). It is beyond the capability of a single monolithic organization to keep at the leading edge of technology in isolation and so the network has become the new organizational form (Jarillo, 1993), not simply a metaphor for organization but the organization itself. Achrol (1997) argues that there are four types of organizational networks: the internal market network, the vertical market network, the intermarket network and the opportunistic network. Such networks are characterized by trust, solidarity, mutuality, flexibility, role integrity and harmonization of conflict.

Participation in networks and/or partnerships is clearly seen by IMI as the most effective mechanism for producing relevant management knowledge. Co-operation with local business, for example, ensures that knowledge is produced in the context of its application, its trans-disciplinarity, flexibility and reflexivity (Gibbons et al., 1994). Co-operation with Western institutions, on the other hand, opens up possibilities to access points of view which may be new and partially or entirely different from local ones. Conflict and communication between such points of view are both necessary and essential if scientific progress is to be achieved (Kuhn, 1962).

Mimi's case is an insightful example of the positive effects networking has upon producing relevant management knowledge. IMI has established an effective network with numerous local organizations such as Bucuria SA (Chocolate factory), "R plus R" SA (Advertising Agency), Anturaj Mobil Group SA (Furniture Factory) as well as banks and government institutions such as: The National Bank of Moldova, The Moldavian Chamber of Trade & Industry, the Agency for Enterprise Restructuring. All these organizations operate an open door policy for project work and research carried out by students and staff. Furthermore, IMI has been an active participant in a number of international networks and partnerships made possible by funding from the British Government, the Eurasia Foundation, the Sores Foundation and, starting from this year, the United States Information Agency. These networks which IMI have developed and from which the current project derives huge benefit are summarized on Figure 1. The network shown is an oversimplified depiction, seeming to indicate one-way communications, albeit passing through two cultural filters. The reality, however, is more complex than can be shown in such a diagram with genuinely multi-directional information and knowledge flows.

It must be stressed that Mimi's participation in such networks has been proactive and dynamic, rather than simply a passive recipient of foreign know-how. IMI has set the agenda themselves (in collaboration with foreign bodies) and has monitored the progress of the various partnerships in an objective and realistic manner. We believe that IMI has been more successful in developing the first indigenous Moldavian MBA programme by adopting the network approach than it could ever have been had it adopted the laissez faire, government control or foreign domination approaches. But it is not simply an institutional achievement. IMI, by virtue of its peculiar positioning has been able to attract, retain and develop the highest calibre individuals and it is through their hard work and dedication that MBA has been so successful.

CONCLUSION

The collapse of communism and adoption by countries such as Moldova of a broadly Western democratic free enterprise business model has coincided with the global revolution in communication and information technologies. Consequent upon their emancipation, Eastern European nations turned, naturally enough, to the West for a model of "how to do business." At that time, the Western democracies were just beginning to realize that the organizational models which had served well enough through most of the 20th century, were perhaps no longer appropriate.

In many industries and situations the management problem has changed radically as already noted. The restatement of the management problem may be something of a simplification since in some areas the old smoke stack industries still survive with the same old problems. However, the nature of work in most industries has been fundamentally altered and as already noted in this paper the organizational form has changed in response to the new technologies.

As old ideas of organization were being challenged by Western theoreticians, politicians in Eastern Europe were overseeing the imposition of such theoretical models both in the public sector and particularly in newly privatized corporations, despite evidence that such ideas were outdated and inefficient. However, it is clear that Western "experts" are not necessarily owners of the most useful "wisdom" in creating local management knowledge for Eastern Europe. Moldova has nevertheless been fortunate that IMI, proactively and critically adopted the networking approach in the development of their MBA program.

NOTE

1. The analysis is based on CISR Economic Survey, April 1999

REFERENCES

Achrol, R. S. (1997), Changes in the Theory of Interorganizational Relations in Marketing. *Journal of the Academy of Marketing Science*, 25 *(1)*, pp. 56-72.
Astley, W. G. and Zammuto, R. F. (1992). Organizational Science, Managers and Language Games. *Organization Science*, 3 (4), pp. 443- 513.

Child, J., & Faulkner, D., (1998), *Strategies of Co-operation: Managing Alliances, Networks and Joint Ventures.* Oxford: Oxford University Press.

CISR Economic Survey, (1999), *Moldova in Transition.* April.

Eisenberg, E. M. and Witten, M. G., (1987), Reconsidering Openness in Organizational Communications. *Academy of Management Review*, 12, 3, 418-426.

Gibbons, M. et al. (1994), *The New Production of Knowledge: The Dynamics of Science and Research in Contemporary Societies.* London: Sage.

Gilbert, K., (2000), "Re-building Babel: The Role of Interpreters in Management Knowledge Transfer in Russia", paper presented at Keele University, March.

Gorman, G., Hanlon D. and King, W. (1997), Some Research Perspectives on Entrepreneurship Education, Enterprise Education and Education for Small Business Management: A ten-year Literature Review. *International Small Business Journal*, 15 (3), pp. 56-77.

Harding, S., (1996). European Expansion and the Organization of Modern Science: Isolated or Linked Historical Processes?. *Organization, 3*(4), pp. 497-509.

Hastings, C., (1993), *The New Organization: Growing the Culture of Organizational Networking.* Maidenhead: McGraw Hill.

Jankowicz, A. D., (1999). Planting a Paradigm in Central Europe: Do We Graft or Must We Breed the Rootstock Anew?. *Management Learning, 30* (3), pp. 281-299.

Jarillo, J. C., (1993), *Strategic Networks: Creating the Borderless Organization.* Oxford: Butterworth Heinemann.

Kelemen, M. (1999). "The Myth of Restructuring, Competent Managers and the Transition to a Market Economy: The Romanian Case." *British Journal of Management, 10* (3), pp. 199-208.

Kelemen, M. and Hristov, L., (1998). From Egalitarian Culture to Entrepreneurial Culture: The Example of Romanian and Bulgarian Organizations. *Journal of Enterprising Culture, 5* (2), pp. 155-170.

Kirzner, I., (1973), *Competition and Entrepreneurship.* Chicago: The University of Chicago Press.

Kostera, M., (1996). "The Manager's New Clothes: on Identity-Transfer in Post-1989," in *Management Education in the New Europe*, Lee, M. et al. (eds.), Thompson Business Press.

Kozminski, A. K., (1996). "Management Education in the Transitional Economies of Central and Eastern Europe," in *Management Education in the New Europe*, Lee, M. et al (eds.), Thompson Business Press.

Kuhn, T. S., (1962, 1970), *The Structure of Scientific Revolutions.* Chicago: The University of Chicago Press.

Kwiatkowski, S. and Saunders, P., (1993), Management Development Assistance for Poland: A Playground for Western Consultants. *Journal of Management Development 12* (1), pp. 56-63.

Lachmann, L.M., (1986), *The Market as an Economic Process.* Oxford: Basil Blackwell.

Likert, R., (1967), *The Human Organization.* New York: McGraw Hill.

Mayo, E., (1945), *The Social Problems of an Industrial Civilization.* Cambridge MA: Harvard University Press.

O'Donoghue, T. A., (1994). Transnational Knowledge Transfer and the Need to Take Cognisance of Contextual Realities. *Educational Review*, 6 (1) pp. 73-89.

O.E.C.D., (1998), *Jobs Strategy Fostering Entrepreneurship*. Paris.

Pearson, G. J., (1999), *Strategy in Action: strategic thinking, understanding and practice*. Harlow: FT Prentice Hall.

Peters, T. and Austin, N., (1985). *A Passion for Excellence: The Leadership Difference*. London: Collins.

Powell, W. W., (1991), "Neither Market nor Hierarchy: Network Forms of Organization" in *Markets, Hierarchies and Networks: The Co-ordination of Social Life*, G. Thompson, J. Frances, R. Levacic and J. Mitchell (eds), London: Sage, pp. 265-277.

Roethlisberger, F., and Dickson, W., (1947), *Management and the Worker*. Cambridge MA: Harvard University Press.

Scarbrough, H., (1996) (eds). *The Management of Expertise*. Basingstoke and London: Macmillan Business.

Thomas, M. J., (1996). "Case Studies as a Management Learning Tool", in *Management Education in the New Europe*, Lee, M. et al (eds.), Thompson Business Press.

MBA Studies in the Czech Republic

Miloslav Kerkovsky
Ladislav Janicek
Milos Drdla

SUMMARY. A survey of MBA study programs in the Czech Republic is presented in this study. The authors share some of their first-hand experience gained during their own teaching in one of the MBA programs. The conclusion presented at the end of the study summarizes their views of developing trends in MBA programs in the Czech Republic. At present, MBA programs are offered by seven teaching institutions in the Czech Republic, three of which provide MBA studies of the American type, four of the European (British) type, and one of the distance-learning type. *[Article copies available for a fee from The Haworth Document Delivery Service: 1-800-HAWORTH. E-mail address: <getinfo@haworthpressinc.com> Website: <http://www.HaworthPress.com> © 2002 by The Haworth Press, Inc. All rights reserved.]*

KEYWORDS. MBA programs, Czech Republic, management education

Miloslav Kerkovsky is affiliated with Brno International Business School, Lipova 41a, CZ-602 00 Brno, Czech Republic (E-mail: kerkovsky@bibs.cz), Ladislav Janicek is affiliated with the Faculty of Mechanical Engineering, University of Technology Brno, Technicka 2, CZ-616 69 Brno, Czech Republic, and Milos Drdla is affiliated with the Faculty of Business and Management, University of Technology Brno, Technicka 2, CZ-616 69 Brno, Czech Republic.

[Haworth co-indexing entry note]: "MBA Studies in the Czech Republic." Kerkovsky, Miloslav, Ladislav Janicek, and Milos Drdla. Co-published simultaneously in *Journal of Teaching in International Business* (International Business Press, an imprint of The Haworth Press, Inc.) Vol. 13, No. 3/4, 2002, pp. 133-156; and: *International Business Teaching in Eastern and Central European Countries* (ed: George Tesar) International Business Press, an imprint of The Haworth Press, Inc., 2002, pp. 133-156. Single or multiple copies of this article are available for a fee from The Haworth Document Delivery Service [1-800-HAWORTH 9:00 a.m. - 5:00 p.m. (EST). E-mail address: getinfo@haworthpressinc.com].

INTRODUCTION

Former Czechoslovakia had a strong record of industrial growth in the interwar period, but if economic recovery is now to be achieved after forty years of a command economy, a huge program of management education has to be undertaken. Much of the management training needed is concerned with the specific functional requirements of different managerial tasks. However, there is a great need not only for differentiated management training, but for integrated programs that give managers a broad overview of how their companies can compete effectively, how to make the most of their resources and opportunities and avoid threats that would expose their weaknesses, and how to manage each area of the business so that it contributes most effectively to the overall success of the enterprise. It may be stated that such programs of managerial education have been in great demand in the Czech Republic during the last decade. For these reasons in particular, several institutions in this Republic succeeded in developing within a relatively short period and in co-operation with foreign universities, the prestigious and internationally recognized Master of Business Administration study program.

MBA study programs represents an internationally recognized standard of academic qualification in the area of management, focusing on the post-graduate development of professional and intellectual skills essential for working in advanced managerial positions. It may even be said that in the course of its development, the MBA has become the standard for top managerial education of its kind. At present, this perception of the MBA exists in the Czech Republic, too, where MBA studies have additionally won the reputation as being one of the most effective means for the re-qualification and adaptation of Czech managers to the conditions of a market economy.

The so-called "Harvard Business Model," inaugurated by the Harvard Business School in the USA (Cameron 1992), can rightly be regarded as the basic pattern against which the study of business administration is generally conducted. There the course comprises an intensive and competitive, full-time, two-year program, the first year of which concentrates on basic management disciplines such as management control, economics, marketing, communication, personnel management and finance. Learning procedures place a great emphasis on case study analyses and corresponding solutions.

In the original American conception, MBA studies were conceived in a classical manner, namely as a two-year postgraduate program tailored primarily to the needs of new university graduates, especially those pursuing the economics track. The classic MBA studies model is distinctly academic and theoretical, with the emphasis placed especially on the analytical-rational profile of managerial skills and the development of mathematical-quantitative reasoning. Therefore, subjects such as financial and operational management dominate American-type MBA studies.

The models used in European institutions closely follow those developed at Harvard. Courses in Europe tend to be designed for the benefit of postgraduate students who would usually have at least three years practical experience in a managerial position. This form of extended study focuses primarily on:

1. Solving practical managerial problems, with special attention directed to the function of Strategic Management, and
2. Developing practical management skills necessary for applying an understanding of business situations to one's management position.

The European conception of MBA studies may be described as a diversified, flexible program lasting for 1-2 years of full-time study, primarily based on teaching methods that emphasize experiential learning, with their dominant focus on developing the efficacy of intellectual and functional managerial skills, and stressing the sociological and psychological elements of managerial abilities. Within this trend, the European type of MBA studies have been shaped markedly by disciplines centring around the management of human resources and personal managerial efficacy, especially in team formation and leadership, and in developing managerial and business communication. This paper presents a survey of MBA studies in the Czech Republic. The authors also share some of their first-hand experience gained during their own teaching of MBA programs. The conclusion sums up their views of the developing trends of this type of course in the Czech Republic.

A SURVEY OF MBA STUDIES IN THE CZECH REPUBLIC

At present, Master of Business Administration[1] studies are offered by seven teaching institutions in the Czech Republic, three of which provide MBA studies of the American type, four of the European (British) type, and one of the distance-learning type. They are surveyed in

Table 1, with more details to be found in the following subsections. These Institutions operate in Prague and Brno, the major industrial and university cities of the Czech Republic. This is primarily due to the accessibility to human and material resources to be found there, together with their strong markets for MBA studies. The institutions and the studies programs are characterized according to the following criteria:

1. The legal status of the institution, its history and co-operation with the foreign university guarantor;
2. The structure of the program and the curriculum;
3. The management of teaching quality and the methods of program delivery;
4. The teaching staff and available resources.

In the Czech Republic, MBA studies are not recognized in the University Law.[2] Therefore Czech universities and other analogous institutions providing education under this law cannot directly organize MBA studies, or if they do, they are not legally able to grant MBA titles. Con-

TABLE 1. Survey of MBA Studies in the Czech Republic*

Institutional organiser of the studies program	Foreign university co-operating partner (guarantor)	Description of the program
U.S. Business School in Prague (since 1990)	College of Business, Rochester Institute of Technology, U.S.A.	Closer to the American model; duration of one year for full-time studies; two to three years for the Executive MBA diploma. 640 teaching units for each of the two versions.
The CMC Graduate School of Business in Celakovice (since 1990)	Joseph M. Katz Graduate School of Business, Pittsburgh University, U.S.A.	Closer to the American model; duration of one year (3 trimesters) for full-time studies and of three years for distance (weekend) studies. The program consists of 678 teaching units.
Prague International Business School (since 1992)	Manchester Metropolitan University, U.K	A combination of the American and the European models; the duration of studies is 4 semesters comprising 657 teaching units. The program is also offered as an "in company" form.
Masaryk Institute for Advanced Studies of the Czech Technical University in Prague (since 1990)	Sheffield Business School, Sheffield Hallam University, U.K.	Closer to the European model; the study is in 3 phases, consisting of three interconnected cycles of gradually increasing difficulty acknowledged by separate certificates. Provided as distance learning, with 4 one-week teaching blocks per year. The duration of each cycle of study is one year.

Institutional organiser of the studies program	Foreign university co-operating partner (guarantor)	Description of the program
Brno Business School of FP VUT in Brno (since 1993)	Nottingham Business School, Nottingham Trent University, Nottingham, U.K.	Closer to the European model. The program is in 3 phases, consisting of three interconnected cycles of gradually increasing difficulty acknowledged by separate certificates. The form of organisation is intensive teaching blocks on weekends, usually once per month. The duration of each level of study is one year.
Open University Foundation in the Czech Republic, in Prague and Brno (since 1993)	Open Business School, Open University of London, U.K.	The program is closer to the European model. It consists of two or three (according to the applicants' previous experience) interconnected cycles of gradually advancing difficulty acknowledged by separate certificates. The form is distance learning. Minimum duration: two years and nine months.
Brno International Business School, Brno	Nottingham Business School, Nottingham Trent University, U.K.	The "Senior Executive MBA" program is closer to the European model. It is tailored to top managerial staff with sufficient work experience and have three interconnected cycles of gradually advancing difficulty acknowledged by separate certificates, each of which lasts for approximately one year. The organisation of the program is adjusted to the needs of the participants, with the curriculum being the same as that of the standard versions. In addition, BIBS is currently preparing a distance-learning program supported by electronic communication for applicants from the countries of the former Soviet block.

Sources: Simberova etal. (1998), Kerkovsky et al. (1998) and Kerkovsky et al. (1999).

sequently, MBA programs here are organized exclusively in co-operation with foreign institutions, the graduation certificates (diplomas and academic titles) being provided by the foreign partner universities. Currently, two American and four British universities contribute to education in the Czech Republic through this form of participation.

As far as British universities are concerned, this co-operation mainly takes the form of so-called validation. The term implies that the course is, in accordance with British law, organized by a validated foreign institution (i.e. a Czech institution in the given case), with the graduation certificates being granted by the British institution that provides the validation. The validation procedure itself is rather demanding in terms of both administrative and time requirements. Its averages duration is more than a year for each institution. It aims firstly to provide a comprehensive assessment of the qualification of the institution being validated to organize the particular type of studies (the so-called Institutional Review) and secondly to assess the studies program itself (Program Review).

No official system currently exists in the Czech Republic for evaluating the image and reputation of individual MBA schools. In dealing with this issue the authors base their judgement, for a particular School, principally on: a human and material resource evaluation, period of operation in the MBA market, demand levels for the product, and reputation of the School's foreign partners. Membership of the Czech Association of MBA Schools (CAMBAS) is also considered to be a significant factor.

U.S. BUSINESS SCHOOL IN PRAGUE

The U.S. Business School was founded in 1990 as a private school supported by the Ministry of Education of the Czech Republic in co-operation with the College of Business, Rochester Institute of Technology, based in Rochester, U.S.A. The school is administered by a Board of Directors consisting of 7 members, all of who are exclusively representatives of RIT and other American universities. The study program was initially developed in co-operation with the School of Economics in Prague but now the partnership is rather formal. The MBA program is provided as a franchise of the RIT MBA program, accredited by the American Assembly of Collegiate Schools of Business, AACSB; the Assembly of University Regents of New York State; and the Middle States Association of Colleges and Schools (MSACS).

The U.S. Business School MBA program comprises 640 teaching units and is provided in two forms: as a 2-semester 40-week full-time studies program consisting of 16 subjects of 40 teaching units each, lasting for approximately 1 year; and as a modular studies program "Executive MBA," instituted in 1995. To achieve the MBA qualification in this form, all 16 modules analogous to the full-time form of studies must be completed. The study of the modular program takes 2-3 years.

The dominant focus of the MBA program is on the subjects of financial administration and accountancy (24%), strategic management (18%), and management economics (18%). Instruction is in English, with certificates granted by Rochester Institute of Technology. The requirements for enrolment into the MBA program are the completion of a university degree (at least of bachelors level) and passing the GMAT (minimum 490 points) and TOEFL (minimum of 550 points) exams.

Nineteen American teachers from Rochester Institute of Technology and other American universities exclusively provide instruction. The school acts as an administrative centre, organizing and administrating the study. The quality of the study program is monitored and controlled by RIT, U.S.A., which takes decisions among other things about the enrolment of each individual student, their financial assistance, granting the degree, and the program content. Students are provided with course literature on an individual basis.

THE CMC GRADUATE SCHOOL OF BUSINESS IN CELAKOVICE

The CMC was founded as an independent educational establishment bearing the legal status of a foundation (non-profit organization) in 1990. The CMC is headed by an international Board of Trustees, having 17 members in 1996 that consists of top representatives from American universities (especially the University of Pittsburgh) and other institutions, as well as American, Canadian and Czech entrepreneurs. The statutory agent is the Dean who is elected by the Board of Trustees; the advisory body is the International Advisory Board comprising (in 1996) approximately 50 members.

The CMC MBA program consists of 678 teaching units. It was instituted as early as in 1991 in co-operation with the Joseph M. Katz Graduate School of Business of University of Pittsburgh, U.S.A., whose study programs have been accredited by the American Assembly of Collegiate Schools of Business. Besides strategic management, the program's dominant focus includes subjects of finance administration, accountancy and marketing. The curriculum includes the completion of a project comprising approximately 25% of the entire course.

Enrolment requirements include holding a university degree, 2 years of work experience, and passing the GMAT and TOEFL exams. The program is offered in two forms: as full-time or as a weekend distance-learning course (WEMBA-Weekend Executive MBA). The full-time course takes 1 year (3 trimesters) while the distance-learning (weekend) program lasts for 3 years. The program concludes with exams taken either at the CMC, to be certified by a CMC diploma, or at the JMK GSB of University of Pittsburgh, where an internationally-recognized MBA diploma of the University of Pittsburgh may be gained. Teaching is conducted in English.

The CMC is an integrated centre of education equipped with modern teaching and accommodation facilities and an integral administrative centre. Its computer equipment and modern didactic technologies reach the standard level. Extremely well equipped is the central library (including the full-text ABI Inform library on CD ROM). The CMC has been registered as a "Center of Excellence" by the U.S. federal government since 1993.

Their teaching staff consists of 16 teachers, 7 of whom are foreign-based (from the University of Pittsburgh and other, mostly American, universities). The Czech members of the teaching staff are internal teachers whose activity at CMC is relatively permanent: about 80% of the Czech teachers have achieved the PhD degree or its equivalent, with 60% holding the pedagogical titles Professor or Docent. The Czech teachers were trained at the University of Pittsburgh between 1990 and 1994.

The CMC has a relatively high prestige in the Czech environment, stemming in particular from its historical publicity. Due to the maintenance of its infrastructure, the school has relatively high fixed costs that are the main cause for the rather high costs for study despite receiving direct and indirect grant support from the U.S.A in particular. Reductions in this financial support, together with the competition presented by other MBA programs in the Czech Republic may result in the ebb of applicants interested in such an expensive study program. As co-operation with American schools is financially very demanding, future restrictions on the participation of foreign teaching staff would not be surprising.

PRAGUE INTERNATIONAL BUSINESS SCHOOL

Prague International Business School was founded as an association in 1992 in co-operation with the Prague School of Economics and the "Management Studies" foundation. Despite its legal independence, the school has close, predominantly professional co-operation with the School of Economics. Its MBA program has been developed under a TEMPUS project in co-operation with three European universities-Manchester Metropolitan University, EADA of Barcelona, and Lancaster University. PIBS is an associate member of the European Foundation for Management Development. The International Academic Board administrates it with 24 members (1996) including representatives (mainly their statutory agents) of European and American universities and business schools. A Dean heads PIBS. The school is essentially an administrative centre, employing several internal teachers who, apart from teaching, also participate in organizing the school's activities.

The MBA program at PIBS was launched in 1993 within the TEMPUS framework. The study program was developed in co-operation with its TEMPUS project partners, particularly Manchester Metropolitan University, which also provides the accreditation. The MBA study is divided into 4 semesters: Semester 1–Basics of Business, Semester 2–Advanced Business, Semester 3–Specialized Blocks, and Semester 4–Project. The program consists of 657 teaching units and is provided in two forms: as a distance/evening course (3 units twice-weekly) and as a full-time (residential) program (with 5 one-week blocks per semester). The distance-learning program is also offered as a special "in-company" program that lasts for two years. The dominant subjects are financial management (12%), operational management (12%), and management of business development (9%). A significant proportion (23%) of the program comprises the projects. The structure of the program is not typical for the British MBA model, but rather reflects the American conception of study. The study program is conceived as a single block leading directly to the award of the MBA diploma. The diploma is granted by Prague International Business School or by Manchester Metropolitan University, according to the type of program.

The enrollment requirements include at least a Bachelors degree from any institution and 3 years of professionally relevant working experience. The entrance procedure, an interview, is of a non-standardized format. Passing GMAT and TOEFL tests is not required. Study is in English and Czech.

Instruction is provided by 29 teachers, mostly members of staff of the School of Economics holding the pedagogical titles Professor or Docent, together with foreign lecturers from the European partner institutions (mainly Manchester Metropolitan University, EADA of Barcelona, Buckinghamshire College, and Lancaster University) as well as professional experts and managers working in industry.

The facilities used by PIBS and its professional standing are closely linked to its co-operation with the Prague School of Economics. However, the school's expenses in connection with its separation from the Prague School of Economics and the attenuation of direct financial support provided by the European programs (TEMPUS), together with ever-growing competition may present a danger, especially where the quality of teaching provided and the accreditation prerequisites are concerned.

MASARYK INSTITUTE FOR ADVANCED STUDIES
OF THE CZECH TECHNICAL UNIVERSITY IN PRAGUE

The Masaryk Institute for Advanced Studies was founded in 1990 as a self-administering branch of the Czech Technical University in Prague (a unit of the Rector's Office) sharing the university's legal status as a state-funded institution, and focusing on life-long learning and postgraduate studies of management and pedagogy. A Director who is appointed by the Rector of the Czech Technical University heads the Institute. The MBA program was instituted in 1992 in co-operation with Sheffield Business School of Sheffield Hallam University, U.K., and with support from the British Council.

The program comprises three phases, taught as interrelated cycles of gradually advancing difficulty and each acknowledged by separate certificates: the Certificate in Management with English (220 teaching units), the Diploma in Management Studies (210 teaching units), and the Master of Administration (325 teaching units). It is provided as a distance-learning program, taught in 4 one-week blocks per year. Each cycle of study lasts for one year. Apart from strategic management, the program's dominant subjects are personnel management (10%) and financial management (9%). A significant part of the program, almost 44%, is taken up by projects and project seminars.

The quality of the MBA program is monitored and controlled by the Award Assessment Board, the academic board of Sheffield Business School, whose president is appointed from the ranks of Sheffield Business School teaching staff. Enrolment requirements include a university degree from any institution and 3 years of managerial experience, with a non-standardized entrance procedure taking the form of an interview. GMAT and TOEFL scores are not required. Study is in English and Czech.

The program has been validated by Sheffield Hallam University, which also grants all the certificates and diplomas. During their studies, students sit exams that are oral, written, or a combination of both, and submit assignments.

A staff of forty-six teachers participate in MBA instruction, with most being external teachers (8 teachers are internal), of whom 16 are foreign-based (predominantly from Sheffield Business School).

BRNO BUSINESS SCHOOL

Brno Business School was founded in 1993 as an institute of the Faculty of Business and Management of the Technical University of Brno, with a focus on life-long learning and postgraduate education in managerial subjects. BBS acts as an administrative centre whose professional standing and facilities are derived from those of the Faculty of Business and Management. As a university organization, BBS shares the legal status of a state-funded institution. The historical roots of BBS and its MBA program however go back as far as 1990, when a TEMPUS project entitled "Brno Business School" was approved, within which the conditions for transferring the MBA program from Nottingham Business School of Nottingham Trent University in England began being prepared. A Director appointed by the Dean of the Faculty of Business and Management of the Czech Technical University of Brno heads BBS. The quality of studies and its long-term development are managed by the Academic Board, whose members are both internal and external, Czech and foreign.

The MBA program comprises three interconnected teaching cycles of gradually advancing difficulty: the Certificate in Management (191 teaching units), the Diploma in Management Studies (230 teaching units), and the Master of Business Administration (166 teaching units). All certificates and diplomas are granted by Nottingham Trent University. Apart from strategic management (16%), the program is dominated in particular by the topics of financial management (15%) and personnel management (12%). A significant part of the program (almost 24%) is taken up by projects and project seminars. The program's structure resembles the British MBA model.

The program is offered through distance learning in the form of a weekend executive program comprising 8-10 weekend teaching blocks per year. Each cycle takes one year. During their studies, students almost exclusively submit assignments pertaining to their own managerial practice.

The enrolment requirements include the successful completion of a university degree without restriction on the institution where this was obtained, 3 years of managerial work experience and a passive knowledge of English (reading, writing, and listening comprehension). The entrance procedure takes the form of an interview. The studies are undertaken in English and Czech, but in the third cycle of study, exclusively in English.

The MBA program teaching staff consists of about 30 teachers of the Faculty of Business and Management of the Technical University of Brno and other Czech universities plus five foreign-based lecturers (mainly from Nottingham Business School). About one third of the core team hold the MBA diploma from Nottingham Business School and 60% of the Czech teaching staff have the title Professor or Docent.

That BBS has the status of a university establishment lends it the advantage of relatively low overheads, which gives this MBA program a strong competitive advantage. The program is relatively advanced and stable, with the most important stabilizing element being the independent internal teaching staff who have an MBA qualification accredited by NBS, with a global competence in providing instruction.

THE OPEN UNIVERSITY FOUNDATION IN THE CZECH REPUBLIC BASED IN PRAGUE AND BRNO

The Open University Foundation in the Czech Republic came into being in 1993, with a legal status as a foundation, although the beginning of the MBA program goes back to 1990. The City University Foundation of Bratislava established in 1990 launched this type of study in the former Czechoslovakia, and subsequently established the OU Foundation in the Czech Republic after the partition of the state. A Director heads the Open University Foundation in the Czech Republic.

The MBA program was instituted in conjunction with the Open University Business School (OUBS) based in Milton Keynes, U.K. The MBA program at OUBS is accredited through the Association of MBAs in the U.K. and franchised to the Open University Foundation via study centres.

The structure of the MBA program offered by the Open University Foundation in Prague is unique, especially since the subjects are combined into interdisciplinary learning modules whose separation into traditional subjects is not really possible. Nevertheless, the program consists of two or three phases: the Professional Certificate in Management (60 credits), the Professional Diploma in Management (60 credits), and finally the Master of Business Administration (120 credits). The 3-phase version is available to applicants over 18 years of age and who have graduated from high school. The 2-phase version presupposes completion of the diploma course "Foundation of Senior Management", in whose Professional Diploma in Management (60 credits) the first two phases of the study are integrated. The 2-phase version may be selected by applicants at least 27 years old having "several" years of managerial experience. The third (MBA) cycle remains the same. The duration of the study differs on an individual basis: the shortest time in which the MBA qualification may be earned is 2 years and 9 months (for the 2-phase version). The usual duration of study however ranges from 4 to 6 years.

The program is offered in the form of distance learning, comprising 9 subjects. It is based on distance-learning texts and audio and video tapes in English and Czech. Only the last cycle of study is exclusively in English. It is primarily gained through self-study and attending regular tutorials given by Czech and English tutors (mainly English in the third cycle of study) that are organized approximately once per month. Students are evaluated on the basis of written exams and assignments. Certification is either by the Open University School or the Open University Foundation in the Czech Republic.

The teaching staff consists of about 30 tutors of whom approximately one half are based in foreign institutions. A network of study centres in Prague, Brno, Ostrava, Opava, Pilsen, Jihlava, Hradec Kralove, and Ceske Budejovice supports instruction.

The issue of efficacy of distance-learning type MBA studies is problematic and remains generally unresolved, especially if we accept the fact that the teaching methods exclude interaction and teamwork. The future of distance-learning methods is seen more in the wider deployment of information technologies and modern methods of so-called interactive distance learning via computer nets, teleconferencing, etc.

BRNO INTERNATIONAL BUSINESS SCHOOL

The Brno International Business School, Inc. (B.I.B.S.) is a private joint-stock company founded with the aim of providing top quality managerial and economic university studies organized through co-operation with foreign universities in Western industrial countries. The inspiration for founding the company in 1998 came from several highly qualified and experienced lecturers engaged in teaching the foreign managerial studies programs that were already in existence in Brno. In organizing its own studies, B.I.B.S collaborates closely with economic- and management-oriented universities in the Czech Republic and abroad. The philosophy of B.I.B.S. consists of supporting and enhancing the development of the entrepreneurial spirit–and consequently also the economical prosperity–of the Moravian region and indeed the whole Czech Republic, by providing managerial education comparable to that in Western industrial countries. Through its educational activities based on international co-operation, B.I.B.S. seeks to encourage its students to develop initiative, rationality, pragmatism, seriousness, and social responsibility.

The MBA Accelerated Executive Program offered at B.I.B.S. comprises 3 phases of interrelated teaching cycles of gradually advancing difficulty acknowledged by the following separate certificates: Certificate in Management (191 teaching units), Diploma in Management Studies (230 teaching units), and Master of Business Administration (166) teaching units). The first two phases of study are provided in Czech, the last one (MBA) in English. The validating institution, Nottingham Trent University, U.K, grants the certificates and diplomas.

The program is dominated by studies of strategic and financial management, human resources management, and informatics. A significant part of the program is taken up by team projects (including an international one). The structure of the program follows that of the British MBA model. The program is offered through distance learning as a weekend executive program with 8-10 intensive weekend modules taught annually. Each cycle lasts for one year. During their studies, students submit assignments in almost all of the teaching blocks that relate to the real environment of their own managerial experience.

The enrolment requirements include a university degree from any type of school, 3 years of managerial experience, plus a passive knowledge of English (reading, writing, and listening comprehension). The entrance procedure takes the form of an interview.

The MBA teaching staff currently consists of approximately 24 teachers active at Czech and foreign universities and about 15 working professionals. Of the core team of Czech teachers, approximately one third have the MBA qualification from Nottingham Business School and 60% hold the title Professor or Docent.

At present, Brno International Business School is preparing in conjunction with its foreign partners Nottingham Trent University and Financial Times Knowledge, the "International Distance Education Master of Business Administration For Central and Eastern Europe" program, designed particularly for participants from the countries of the former Soviet Block. The program is being prepared as a distance-learning program, to be supported by (a) contact centres in the target countries, and (b) electronic communication.

Besides MBA studies, B.I.B.S. also offers other programs validated by foreign universities, namely the "MSc in Management" and the "BA HONS in Business Management" programs.

MBA PROGRAMS IN THE CZECH REPUBLIC–A SUMMARY

In the Czech Republic, MBA studies are currently offered in multiple forms and variants, with the individual programs differing substantially. In some instances, they can hardly be described as following either the American or the European model. In addition, as a general rule, the process of its genesis, the framework within which it is provided, and the legal status of the institutions providing it have affected the conception of the program. On the basis of analysis conducted on this (Janicek 1997 and Simberova 1998) the following conclusions can be formulated:

1. The quality and level of sophistication of MBA programs in the Czech Republic is reflected in their varying levels of accreditation (validation). Differing interpretations of the concept of "accreditation" by the individual institutions tend to result in a distorted picture of the actual quality of the programs. Relatively good quality is usually found in those schools where accreditation is provided by renowned foreign universities.
2. The stability of MBA programs is generally quite low. It is principally the MBA programs of those institutions whose financial support from various foreign programs and projects of support has been reduced that are becoming rather unstable. This situation has to a certain extent also been caused by the non-existence of relevant legislation and a considerable dependence of the individual MBA programs on the accreditation-providing institution. This dependence is mostly rather costly, which in the case of some of the institutions has led to the launching of MBA programs of their own without, or with only limited, participation and warrant of quality by the foreign partner. With the non-existence of a legislation-based accreditation in the Czech Republic, this causes a certain devaluation of the MBA qualification in this country.
3. Because of their differing histories, the compatibility of the individual MBA programs offered in the Czech Republic is very low and problematic. There are 7 institutions providing MBA

studies in 6 different forms. Resemblances between these conceptions and a degree of compatibility can be found only among the MIAS, BBS, and BIBS programs. In this respect, the considerable dependence of the client on any one school and its MBA program becomes a problem, with a change in school being complicated by the incompatibility of the curricula and the program lay-outs and formats.

4. The dominant format is distance learning, although some of the institutions are starting to implement such courses based on modern conceptions of distance learning with the support of electronic communication. As an example we may cite the example of the "International Distance Education Master of Business Administration for Central and Eastern Europe" program, being prepared by BIBS in co-operation with its foreign partners.

5. The quality of the teaching staff is the key factor in determining the quality of the program. In most institutions, the teaching staff unfortunately consists mainly of external teachers and this considerably complicates the development and consequently also continuity in developing MBA programs. Besides that, a reduction in the participation by foreign teachers diminishes links with the parental institution, and this in turn reduces the prestige, and in many cases also the professional credibility, of the program.

THE CZECH ASSOCIATION OF MBA SCHOOLS

In parallel with a number of other European countries, MBA studies in the Czech Republic are not included into the university system of education whose quality has been warranted by the state. Research (Janicek 1997) shows that not even Czech experts place MBA studies within the university system of education. The MBA is generally perceived as neither replacing the B.A. nor the technical M.A. level of university education in this Republic. It is instead seen as being a life-long education program. After gaining some, usually three-years of work experience, university graduates of all specializations working in managerial positions may find it a useful further education of a good quality that is highly relevant to their progress in their managerial careers.

The absence of an official body responsible for maintaining the quality of MBA programs in the Czech Republic necessitated the founding of the Czech Association of MBA Schools (CAMBAS) whose role is to provide, maintain, and develop the high standard and prestige of MBA programs in this country. The association came into being with the support of a European Union grant in 1998.[2]) Another reason for founding the CAMBAS association was the need to have an institution that could act as a partner for analogous foreign institutions such as AACSB in the U.S.A., AMBA in Great Britain, and FIBAA in Germany, Austria and Switzerland. CAMBAS also wishes to be a partner of the European Foundation for Management Development (EFMD) in Brussels that guarantees the quality of MBA studies throughout Europe.

CAMBAS has also set tasks for itself in the area of the further development of MBA programs in the Czech Republic. For this purpose, the association each year organizes scholarly conferences and seminars in which MBA lecturers, working professionals as well as Czech and foreign students participate. In order to raise the quality of MBA studies, CAMBAS intends to assess the individual schools in the Czech Republic and to regularly publish their assessments in relevant journals. These assessments will also include an evaluation of MBA graduates by their employers.

CAMBAS membership is accessible only to those institutions whose MBA programs have been accredited in accordance with CAMBAS accreditation regulations derived from accreditation regulations of MBA associations in industrial countries, particularly the U.S.A. and Great Britain. The accreditation criteria of the EFMD have also been used as a model. The accreditation committee consisting of top experts who, apart from teaching in the domain of management at the university level, are also required to have long-standing MBA teaching experience, including teaching abroad where possible, conducts the accreditation procedure.

CAMBAS has been recognized by the Ministry of Education, Sport and Youth of the Czech Republic as a partner for warranting the quality of MBA programs. Experts increasingly perceive CAMBAS membership as a mark of quality.

A COMPARISON OF THE TEACHING OF MBA AND SIMILAR COURSES PROVIDED BY CZECH UNIVERSITIES

In this section, the authors of the present paper share their experience accumulated during the course of their long-standing teaching activities in traditional managerial studies and MBA programs in the Czech Republic.

The MBA, compared to similar courses provided by Czech universities (i.e. traditional managerial studies) differs substantially in its use of a broad range of teaching methods. Teaching in the MBA is through a combination of lectures, seminars, discussions, case study analyses, simulations and managerial games; group working activities, intensive residential meetings and industrial visits. Most importantly, the MBA students are expected not only to learn from their teachers, but also to exchange their knowledge and experiences with their colleagues.

MBA students must make a great effort to work by themselves under the guidance of, and with assistance from, their lecturers. They need to independently manage their work and directly connect it to their practical experience wherever possible. We must learn from the MBA in more traditional managerial studies in making better use of the methods of teamwork and the application of case studies to our classes. Our students, like the MBAs, must learn to analyze problems, to formulate proposals about how to treat them and–something which is especially important in managerial profession–to argue for them and to motivate people into implementing them. Students must be educated with the aim of learning how to decide for themselves in an optimal way but at the same time they must be prepared to bear their own responsibility for the agreed decisions and to realize fully their consequences. We also have to pay greater attention to the human dimension and ethics of entrepreneurial activities.

The MBA curriculum, in comparison with similar studies in CR, also differs quite a lot. In the first stage it is primarily courses of Personal Effectiveness, Environment of the Manager and Managing People that are included in the study program. This is evidence of a strong emphasis on an as rapid as possible acquisition of personal communicative and managerial skills in preparation for the further development of consecutive parts of the Integrated MBA study. MBA students prepare their study plan with the help of their tutors at the outset, which is very unusual from the viewpoint of our educational system that has survived from the era of the centrally managed society. This plan is based on the students' individual needs and enables them to participate in forming the study.

Many out-of-school activities, especially industrial visits, are included in the MBA study program from the beginning. Compared to the conception of industrial visits in traditional studies in CR, the MBA industrial visits differ substantially by their strong purposeful orientation. They are focusing primarily on a team evaluation of the company's strategy and the efficiency of the management of companies visited. This is also a good opportunity for the students to realize the importance of teamwork and to broaden their ability to participate in it. The aim of developing their ability to gather and analyze information is also very important. For instance, a quite common task for a group of three to five students during the two-day excursion would be to prepare a group presentation dealing with a strategic analysis and formulation of conclusions for the further development of the company visited.

At the end of the study a special Residential Week is organized in collaboration with the foreign partners. This is an excellent opportunity for the students to gain alternative perspectives on the management of companies in other countries of Europe.

Critical to the success of the MBA program is the use of interactive methods of teaching and learning, especially with the case study approach. The method of teaching through the use of extended case studies is highly effective for the following reasons in particular:

1. It is attractive to both students and teachers. For the staff, the way that the case develops in class can never be fully anticipated. Each group of students will bring their own, potentially unique blend of experience and insight to bear on the case. In using cases, teachers are always likely to be challenged and learn much from the observations of managers on the course. For students it is a welcome contrast from lectures that provide the authoritative position on any matter under consideration. Students have to take some of the responsibility for their own learning, a key element of the MBA philosophy, and are stimulated by competing with each other to provide the most cogent analysis. Thus it is an approach that encourages learning.

2. The analytical framework of the MBA works very well in the Central European context. For instance, the module "Meeting Customers Needs" requires course members to focus on what the customers of a company are really looking for and how to produce goods and services that truly correspond with consumer demand. How consumer demand is constituted has to be identified locally, though guidance is given from the analytical framework as to how to conceptualize this and measure it, e.g. in terms of lowest cost, quick service, particular types of product differentiation, etc. Intensive discussion of such factors in the local context gives students an understanding of the busi-

ness environment that would have prevented costly business failures that occur through incorrect assumptions.

3. The case study approach stretches Czech managers in important ways, not just in terms of what they understand but what they are comfortable with. In particular, Czech managers quickly develop the skills of strategic analysis of firms and practice this skill with great effectiveness. But they are much less comfortable identifying solutions for business problems for which there is no "right" answer, beyond that which is argued for most effectively. Over the past forty years Czech managers have had little to gain from proposing creative solutions to business problems, and they have little experience of the potential of outcomes that might be planned for. Nevertheless, this is a most valuable skill and requires experience and confidence as well as insight.

4. By basing much of the analysis of managerial situations on real life, either in the companies in which managers on the course work or else through looking at case studies based on real situations, students are able to better develop a general intuitive understanding of what works in the Czech business environment, as opposed to that which textbooks from North America or Western Europe might imply.

For example, the Western management literature indicates that large firms dominate small firms in the buyer-supplier relationship. However this assumes that large firms are strong and well organized. In the emerging market economies of Central and Eastern Europe there are opportunities for well organized small and medium sized firms to play the leading role, using large firms which are having difficulty coming to terms with the new business context as their subcontractors to do the manufacturing and assembling for them (Kerkovsky and Jemelik 1996). Given the nature of the business environment in such transitional economies, it is more advisable to build up generalizations based on local experience than to rely on theories premised on untested assumptions drawn from the West.

CONCLUSION

Companies operating in the Czech Republic face a very different business environment in comparison to that which they experienced under the period of state socialism. In order to survive the national, and indeed international competition that they now frequently face, they often need to make strategic changes to their products, their markets, their processes, their staffing, their systems and their financing.

On the other hand there are many developments that show that Czech managers are quick to learn and practice the new rules of the game. The new MBA has already proved that it can provide the insights and skills that are needed to deal with the new situation. For example, within the Technical University Brno, taking the MBA program as students has already led senior management teachers to create a new structure for providing business and management education (the Faculty of Business and Management and Brno Business School), new products (including a version of the MBA adapted to the Czech environment), new processes (interactive education), a newly qualified staff and new financial arrangements (development costs from the EC followed by fees from course members). It has been tested in the market and found acceptable. Similar developments have been taking place within companies as a result of participation in the program. Czech business managers have been increasingly aware of the fact that it is especially themselves who must rationalize the management of their businesses and that MBA studies, by embracing practical and realistic task solving, can be the ideal means to help them achieve that end. In the Senior Executive MBA program at Brno International Business School for example (see section 2.7) the established practice is that the students–as top managers–deal with particular real-life problems from the environment of their own businesses within the framework of their final projects, under the supervision of experienced lecturers. The school of course guarantees that the information conveyed in this way will not be misused.

There is also great value in using the MBA-type approach to achieve similar kinds of change in the sphere of the public administration sector (e.g. local and city councils, hospitals) to give a clearer understanding of how to use available resources most effectively in providing an optimal range of services. Indeed, a public sector route through an MBA degree, concentrating on issues of particular concern in public administration is now quite common.

The future of managerial education is determined by a number of factors reflecting not only the technological progress that relates to the massive influx of information technology into society, but also the increasingly global and international character of business and management. The future conceptions and trends in managerial education including MBA studies are likely to be a search for a compromise between such aspects as:

1. The need to learn from local environments vs. the growing impact of the global environment;
2. The management of international alliances and corporations vs. the necessity of maintaining a distinct institutional culture for the establishment;
3. The launching of multimedia technologies vs. the need to developing interpersonal skills;
4. The networked distribution of co-operating establishments vs. the need for a centre of education;
5. The creation of business school consortia at national and international levels in preparation for the internationalization of the studies;
6. The trend of switching from standardized to interactive programs tailored specifically to individual client needs;
7. The trend towards executive programs that combine learning with a direct use of the students' experience;
8. The increasing importance of the distance-learning format of studies in combination with the assistance of interactive multimedia technologies;
9. The increasing importance of interdisciplinary interaction in the portfolio of managerial skills;
10. The fact that the future is associated with virtual business schools, based on the virtual integration of distributed resources and a network of co-operating establishments via multimedia technologies, using the interactive formats of distance-learning.

The ability to flourish in competition will be based especially on aspects such as the following:

1. Partnership with the client;
2. Superior education technologies and technical support;
3. Implementing modern teaching methods based on experiential learning;
4. High competence and professionalism in providing education including the participation of experts in the profession;
5. A certified quality.

These aspects are undoubtedly going to affect the future of MBA studies in the Czech Republic, too. The parallel existence of several different models for MBA may be expected to complement the standard MBA models and simultaneously reflect new trends such as:

1. A broader spread of the International MBA model;
2. Combining MBA studies with other professional specializations;
3. A wider spread of the Executive MBA model as a prestigious format for such studies;
4. Widening the possibilities for advanced MBA specializations (in the form of electives);
5. Amplification of MBA programs taught in intensive blocks.

The global trend in MBA studies will probably be directed towards integration based on the development of supranational and transcultural features of the programs. In this context, establishing supranational structures for controlling the quality of studies may be expected, too. With respect to the internationalization of education and the establishment of an internationally-recognized credit system, MBA studies stand a good chance of becoming the first world-wide qualification standard for top managerial education to be developed.

NOTES

1. For the purposes of this paper, MBA studies are defined as courses with more than 600 units of direct teaching, or, for distance-learning, their equivalent. Apart from these courses, some markedly shorter courses (ranging around 200 units of teaching) are offered in the Czech Republic by several institutions under the label of MBA studies. They are, however, not considered as MBA studies in this work.

2. University Law including amendments of other laws of April 22, 1998, of the Statute Book of the Czech Republic.

REFERENCES

Cameron, S. (1992) *The MBA Handbook: An Essential Guide to Effective Study*. London: Pitman Publishing.

Janicek, L. (1997) *Conception and Development of the MBA Studies within the Educational System of the Czech Republic*. Brno, Brno Business School, MBA dissertation.

Kerkovsky, M. et al. (1998) *MBA Validation Document.* Brno Business School, Faculty of Business and Management, University of Technology Brno.

Kerkovsky, M. et al. (1999) *MBA Annual Report 1999.* Brno International Business School, annual report.

Kerkovsky, M. and Jemelik, V. (1996) *Tosca Ltd. A Case Book.* edited by Graham Beaver and David Jennings, Nottingham Business School, PC DIR, Brno, ISBN 80-85895-10-2.

Simberova, I. et al. (1998) *An Analysis of MBA Studies in CR.* Brno, Business and Management Faculty, University of Technology Brno, research report.

Index

157

Printed in the United States
by Baker & Taylor Publisher Services